CAMBRIDGESHIRE

Edited by Lynsey Hawkins

First published in Great Britain in 2003 by
YOUNG WRITERS
Remus House,
Coltsfoot Drive,
Peterborough, PE2 9JX
Telephone (01733) 890066

HB ISBN 0 75434 311 1
SB ISBN 0 75434 312 X

FOREWORD

This year, the Young Writers' The Write Stuff! competition proudly presents a showcase of the best poetic talent from over 40,000 up-and-coming writers nationwide.

Young Writers was established in 1991 and we are still successful, even in today's modern world, in promoting and encouraging the reading and writing of poetry.

The thought, effort, imagination and hard work put into each poem impressed us all, and once again, the task of selecting poems was a difficult one, but nevertheless, an enjoyable experience.

We hope you are as pleased as we are with the final selection and that you and your family continue to be entertained with *The Write Stuff! Cambridgeshire* for many years to come.

CONTENTS

St Bede's School, Cambridge

The Poems

A HAPPY WORLD

We eat, we sleep, we laugh and cry
We do what we can every day to get by.
We teach, we learn, we make, we earn
We do what we can to be strong, to be stern.

We hurt, we fight, we help and give
We sing and pray and can forgive.
We live, we die, we love and try
To make our lives worth living.

But then there's the bad, who make people sad
Murder and killing, life-shattering, blood-spilling
If we can't live in peace, how can we live?
We must learn to love and start to forgive.

But until we mature and realise violence is wrong
We will never escape the true fact it's lifelong
So just think of the millions suffering right now,
But be strong and forget, because you're safe in *your* world,
Where you're happy and giving and making your life worth living.

Katherine Ann Kerry

SEPTEMBER 11TH 2001

It was September the 11th 2001
A year ago when the world went numb.
The air was crisp, the sky was blue.
Out of the sky an aeroplane flew.
In a flash it crashed.
Dust filled the air.
Thousands looked up in despair.
Within an hour it happened again.
Thousands of people were instantly slain.
For those that survived to tell their tale,
About the seconds they visited Hell.
For those that didn't, their families say,
That in the end the whole world will pay.

James Goodfellow (11)
Bottisham Village College

9/11 BALLAD

A normal day
That seemed so positive,
If only they knew
Oh, what would happen
Oh, what would happen.

Over the horizon
Loomed the jet,
A normal jet
Or so it seemed
Or so it seemed.

As the jet
Headed for Manhattan,
The towers seemed
So sturdy and strong
So sturdy and strong.

As the pedestrians heard
The plane overhead,
It crept towards the towers
With engines roaring
With engines roaring.

Into the tower
The plane did plunge,
With screams and cries
From the people below
From the people below.

It seemed so horrific
People jumped for their lives,
Out of the buildings
To the streets below
To the streets below.

As the second tower
Cringed in fear,
It had no idea
Of what was to come
Of what was to come.

As the second jet
Broke the skyline,
The workers looked out
They knew what was coming
They knew what was coming.

The second plane
Braced itself for the crash.
Through the tower
It thrust itself
It thrust itself.

An hour passed
And then it happened,
Those formidable towers
Began to fall
Began to fall.

As a storm of debris
Fell to the streets,
Frantic civilians
Ran for their lives
Ran for their lives.

All that was left
Of those great robust towers,
Was a graveyard of workers
And a burning fire
And a burning fire.

Sam Riches (11)
Bottisham Village College

A Tragic Loss, They Thought

He was a great, great soldier
Who'd spent many years at war,
He received a letter one day
And knew exactly what it was for,
It was for his loving wife
They'd been married for three years, nearly four.

He handed it to his wife
She opened it with a knife,
It looked like an invitation,
It was a sensation.

It was from an old friend from school
She lived in Liverpool,
But Sarah wasn't sure,
She thought it may be a bit of a bore.

But Rob was sure,
It wouldn't be a bore,
Rob forced her to go,
So she decided to go.

It was about a hundred miles
But when she got there, there were all smiles,
At the party she had a good time,
She was the champ of mimes.

She was driving in her car
And she hadn't gone far,
Before there was a crash
And an enormous bash.

Rob thought Sarah was dead
She'd seriously damaged her head,
It was looking dull,
Sarah had fractured her skull.

Rob was very surprised
When Sarah turned up one day,
'I thought you had died!'
'I'm not dead!'
Rob was delighted,
The doctor must have lied!

Daniel Pearce (11)
Bottisham Village College

SECOND WORLD WAR

Guns firing day and night
Hitler dictating to the innocent Germans
Killing for no reason.

Nurses cleaning up blood from
the wounded British soldiers.
There's another war up in the air,
people dying at speeds of 150mph,
crashing to the floor
blowing up some of the buildings
and people stationed on the ground.

Six years of war plus a few months.
Thousands of people leaving this Earth
for the heavens.
People being tortured in concentration
camps by gassing and starvation.

You would see the planes flying overhead
and you wouldn't know whether they
were yours or the enemy's.
Bombs were dropping day and night
people dying and gas lingering in the air.

Conor McCabe (11)
Bottisham Village College

THE WAR'S GAIN IS A LOVER'S LOSS

The door slowly creaks to open,
There he is standing in the door frame,
As she walks in,
He slowly whispers her name.

His clothes, so clean and crisp,
Her heart, so warm with love,
As they sit down,
They hear the loving coo of a dove.

A dove bringing peace,
From the war so strong and clear,
Each night as a bomb rings out
And sounds ever so near.

The time has come,
To say goodbye,
The sadness comes and
They both start to cry.

Both faces turn grey with fear,
Hearts are broken,
Empty, clear.

The war, destructive,
Cities wiped out,
The love, the passion,
Everyone goes without.

The nights pass,
The fear grows,
Where is her love?
Nobody knows.

A knock on the door,
Bad news, she thought,
A soldier standing there,
Strictly taught.

An envelope resting,
Under his arm,
She slowly takes it,
Her heart, anything but calm.

His death so public,
His friends and family shocked,
Her heart no longer broken,
But firmly locked.

Emma Louise De Meyer (11)
Bottisham Village College

THE WAR

Women are scared as their men leave to fight,
streets are deserted, there's no one to find
because they're hiding from the terror.

Bombs are dropping, gunshots are fired
lights are flashing as the night goes on
there's not a scrap of food for anyone.

Army troops are fighting for their country,
planes fill the sky, wherever you look
battleships are sailing away in the distance.

Speeches are made as the battle goes on
in this everlasting war,
battles are won and also lost,
but the war goes on strong

Invasions coming from across the sea,
everyone's scared as they hide,
tanks fill the streets of the city
as the battle rages on all night.

Josh Curry (11)
Bottisham Village College

THE BALLAD OF TIA MARIA

Tia was my kitten.
The first kitten who was mine, all mine.
I knew her all her life, I chose her right from the start.
Tia was my kitten.

Tia was the most beautiful kitten I have ever seen.
She never grew that big,
But she had the biggest personality I've ever known.
She was a little menace, but we loved her all the same.

She grew boisterous and adventurous,
Then she got sick.
Bit by bit she struggled through,
But it was all in vain.

She made it through her first Christmas,
But in February she lost the fight.
She passed away whilst fast asleep.
Tia was my kitten.

We missed her so,
We mourned for our little tortie kitten,
Things looked dark,
When suddenly someone turned on a light!

Bilbao was that someone, he took Tia's place.
He isn't a replacement, just someone new.
Tia stays in our hearts.
Tia was my kitten.

Emma Whitehead (11)
Bottisham Village College

SEPTEMBER 11TH

This is the day that the world shall remember
Where fear struck our hearts
It sent shivers down our spines
And made the whole world stop.

So many died a terrible death
The planes full of people
Explosions and fires
The terror so gripping
As the Twin Towers crumbled to the ground.

Screaming and shouting
Dust covering the streets
All the sirens and flashing lights
The brave firemen trying to save so many people

A month later . . .
And the army started looking for the terrorist
They ended up with a man
A man who lives in Afghanistan
A man by the name of bin Laden.

A year later . . .
They have still not found him
Some people think he killed himself
But nobody knows for sure
Could there be others who follow in his footsteps?

Laura Durrant (11)
Bottisham Village College

THEY'RE IN LOVE

A girl called Elizabeth had a big crush
And whenever she thought about him she would blush.
Ben, the boy that she fancied, also fancied her
And everything seemed to be a great big blur.

One day they found themselves staring into each other's eyes.
About a week later, decided to talk and they realised

Chorus
Ooh I'm in love, I'm in love, come on, come on, you know what
I'm talking about.
Ooh, I'm in love, I'm in love

Before they knew it, they were going out
And they couldn't even hear themselves shouting out.

Ooh I'm in love, I'm in love, come on, come on, you know what
I'm talking about.
Ooh, I'm in love, I'm in love.

After a while, Ben had to move away
And Elizabeth did not know what to say
It felt like the best journey of her life,
But then a brick wall, a dead end, a red light.

When Ben got to his new home, he felt lonely and he
couldn't understand why.
Then he realised it was because he had said goodbye.

Ooh I'm in love, I'm in love, come on, come on, you know what
I'm talking about.
Ooh, I'm in love, I'm in love.

So Ben went back to her
Elizabeth thought that something had occurred to her
The brick wall now had a gap in it, so she went to the other side
And then she looked to see who she was standing beside.

*Ooh I'm in love, I'm in love, come on, come on, you know what
I'm talking about.
Ooh, I'm in love, I'm in love.*

But to whom she said . . .

*Ooh I'm in love, I'm in love, come on, come on, you know what
I'm talking about.
Ooh, I'm in love, I'm in love.*

To him!

Royal Hersel (11)
Bottisham Village College

THE LITTLE GREEN MAN

There was a little green man
who loved his little green mouse.
They both lived together
in a little green house.

One day the little green man went out
leaving little green mouse inside.
When he came back, little mouse had gone
and the little green man sat down and cried.

He loved his mouse,
because he was so funny and cute.
Suddenly he heard a noise,
and out popped his mouse from an old boot.

The little green mouse jumped out of the boot
and ran towards the door.
But the little green man saved him in time
and they lived happily forever more.

Jack Ison (11)
Bottisham Village College

HOLLY AND JESSICA

People talking, eating, laughing, sitting in the summer sun,
Family feasting, children playing, fun and games for everyone,
Two young girls leave all alone,
Say no goodbyes, just take their phones,
They disappear without a trace,
Posters everywhere show their face,
The nation is left wondering.

People searching hedges, rivers, looking for the two best friends,
Family crying, people trying, hoping that their hearts will mend,
False alarms, sightings abound,
Maybe the two will soon be found,
The parents say, 'Please send them home.'
No greater love could they have shown,
The nation is left praying.

People finding clothes and earth mounds,
Newspapers offering thousands of pounds,
Only the gamekeeper finds them for real,
Nothing but bones, how must he feel?
Everyone arrives at the funeral of the girls,
Dressed, looking happy, bright colours and pearls,
The nation is left weeping.

People coping, helping, caring, getting back to daily life,
Children going back to school, even after all the strife,
A man is charged, a woman too,
Police are still hunting for another clue,
Children run free but at what cost?
The nation is left reflecting.

Sophie Millard (11)
Bottisham Village College

OMAH BEACH

The boat was swaying from side to side,
in the boat, many American soldiers hoping to survive.

One of them, Private John Castle,
number 078655, belonged to Squadron 109,
brought up in Louis Reⱴ:a, called up just last week.

Suddenly the boat stopped at Omah Beach,
two big fortified posts waiting for American meat.

For a split second, nothing happened,
then *rat-ta-ta-tat,* the guns went off,
many died before stepping ashore.

Bullets were flying everywhere,
shouts and screams everywhere,
but John managed to scramble into a hole,
his best friend, Max Smith, drowned in the water,
bullets injured him but 30% were killed in the water.

America was a sitting duck,
it seemed the Germans had the luck but somehow
they missed the Bangalore man.

The Bangalore man made it to the wire,
placed them in the sand, 1, 2, 3,
Bang! Went the land.

The soldiers made it to the posts,
blew them up too.
The Americans made it to the top.

They won the battle but just by an inch.
Thousands died in the line of fire.
Many more from their injuries, yet it was tough.
Yes, many died but in the end it helped millions of other to survive.

Joe Griffiths (11)
Bottisham Village College

THE SHOW

It's two days left to the show
But am I ready to go?
His mane's all matted
And soon to be plaited
And tied up in a bow!

It's one day left to the show
And I'm still not ready to go.
His tail's all tangly
Looks all mangly
And hanging really low!

It's half a day left to the show
And I'm nearly ready to go
He's all covered in dust
And needs a good brush
Until he shines aglow!

It's the morning of the show
And I'm about ready to go
I need to shower
Give me half an hour
To get dressed in my clothes!

I'm driving to the show
And I'm more than ready to go
He looks really lovely
Neat, nice and bubbly
Looks like he's ready to flow!

I'm riding around in the ring
Oh, look at me, I sing
A girl just fell,
Before the last bell
What bad luck, *ding, ding, ding!*

There are two of us now at the last
But who will be best of class?
It's time for the jump
Oh, she's hit a bump
I've now got to go really fast.

Looks like I am the winner!
Then off to a big, slap-up dinner.
For me and my Noddy,
We never act shoddy!
Thank goodness, I'm no beginner!

Georgina Leggatt (11)
Bottisham Village College

CASSIE

When I first saw her,
I was sure that I loved her.
She was cute and cuddly,
Small and bubbly.
She was as black as soot,
Now it hurts when she squashes my foot.
She's got soppy eyes and floppy ears,
But Cassie has no fears.

When something's wrong,
She comes along,
To make me feel strong.
Cassie loves her squeaky paper,
I love to play with her.
She scavenges for her bouncy ball,
And finds it after all.
Cos she's potty and round the bend,
Cassie's adventures will never end!

Amanda Milly Ticehurst (11)
Bottisham Village College

THE SECOND WORLD WAR

The dark streets, lonely and desolate
Grey fumes linger, wafting from a fresh crater in the street,
The food is mouldy, rations are small, we save all the food we can.

Tape over windows, a feeble attempt at hiding the cracks,
Planes fly overhead, spraying their metal cargo.
They fall in sheets, like the cruel, sharp rain.
The explosions lighting the streets, the rain is lightening.

The gas masks are worn,
They are hot, smelly, sticky and uncomfortable,
But they save us from the deadly fumes,
We hope, we pray.

Children torn away from their parents,
Many never to see either again.
Toys lie in the street,
To be loved no more.

The shelters are crowded,
Cheery music disguises the depression.
The gloomy shelters become happy, the thought of bombs forgotten
                                            for a little while,
But the bombs fall, children cry!

Caitlin Chapman (11)
Bottisham Village College

THE SECOND WORLD WAR

I was flying a plane in the Second World War
Millions of planes flying around
Planes were dropping millions of bombs, just like millions of stones.
Houses were exploding and lots of places were destroyed into
                                            little pieces.
People were screaming and escaping.
Some children were crying on the streets waiting for bombs to hit them.

Planes were exploding every moment in the sky.
Captains busy talking with the soldiers about how to fight.
I was dropping millions of bombs
To hit houses and lots of places.
Suddenly a plane hit my plane by accident
And we exploded together!

Kei-Wai-Sin (11)
Bottisham Village College

BALLAD

Saddam Hussein is the leader,
The dictator who tortures and kills,
Anyone who dares speak against him
Has their fate lying in his will.

America thinks we are terrorists,
Building weapons to attack,
Like that Osama bin Laden
But confidence is what we lack.

The Americans need a lot of help,
They can't do this on their own,
That's why they've asked Britain to help,
But Britain will not do this alone.

Britain will not do it unless the United Nations help,
They will not attack unless they do,
But some of the countries are declining,
The Americans are hoping they will agree soon.

My people are waiting in anxiety,
To hear the important news,
We listen out for bulletins,
To see if we can find any clues.

Vicki Hodgson (11)
Bottisham Village College

HOLLY AND JESSICA

Holly and Jessica lived in Soham,
At only ten years old.
They supported Manchester United,
Wearing their red shirts, they never said goodbye.

Their worried parents prayed for news.
Their pictures shown around the world,
Hopes and fears mixed with tears.
Parents everywhere watching children.

As the days passed we hoped till the last
For any evidence, just a shred.
Then news that we all did dread.
Prayers and heartfelt wishes said.

But still the question does remain,

Why?

Arthur Savory (11)
Bottisham Village College

DIANA'S DEATH

Diana's death was a great shock to all
She was a kind and loving person
She never deserved to die
She never deserved to die

She died with her friend,
Both so happy and young
So innocent was she
So innocent was she

She was a mother to two
She loved them to bits
So sad the world was when she was gone
So sad the world was when she was gone

She had no fear
To touch the untouchable
A queen she was, without a crown
A queen she was, without a crown.

Julia Saville (11)
Bottisham Village College

SEPTEMBER 11TH

It was a normal day in New York
but no one knew the disaster that was about to occur
one that bin Laden had been planning!

People stared as the first plane hit the buildings
and as pieces flew out of the buildings
and then before they knew what was happening
a second plane hit the other tower.

As the second plane hit the tower,
people ran down the stairs with hope in their hearts
that they would see their loved ones again.

As the tower collapsed, glass flew everywhere,
bricks and steel hit the ground and piled up
as police and firemen got ready to look for survivors.

As the dust settled, police and firemen looked for survivors
and citizens joined in to help.

Sean Robert Russell   (10)
Bottisham Village College

THE LONELY SNAIL

I walk around all day and night,
Upset, lonely and tired,
The sunlight shining down so bright,
No frost and rain in sight,
No frost and rain in sight.

Searching for scraps of food on the ground,
But it's no use,
No food to be found,
I just want to curl up and stay in my home,
But not on my own,
But not on my own.

Poor and cold,
I have to struggle on,
Waiting, just waiting,
For the night to come on,
For the night to come on.

One day I woke up
And sat up yawning,
I looked out of the window,
And saw someone crawling,
And saw someone crawling.

I took a closer look,
It was a beautiful lady,
Before I knew it there was a knock at my door,
This lady I had
Never seen before,
Never seen before.

'I'm home,' she yelled,
'Back in my lonely house,'
She didn't notice she went through the wrong door,
And then we met,
For the first time,
For the first time.

'Who are you?' I cried,
'I'm just a lonely snail with nothing to hide,'
She replied,
She replied.

So from then on we became partners,
Did everything together,
So I'm not a lonely snail anymore,
So I'm not a lonely snail anymore.

Laura Haird (11)
Bottisham Village College

THE BIKER MAN

A bike is coming, coming for goods
Quick hide, it's the Biker Man
In a flame-red suit with a thunder helmet.

An old man with dirty grey clothes was out
The Biker went as fast as a click of a finger
The old man lost his money and more
He was down on the floor.

The police came after the Biker Man
They blocked him off so well he shot them
He came on his fire bike and stole more
Police got so scared they wouldn't venture out.

That day the Biker Man's bike broke down
Police went and found him
They shot and shot
And in the end, they caught him.

Dean William Hilborn (11)
Bottisham Village College

THE WRIGHT BROTHERS

Our first flight was in daylight
the plane went up, up, up
and when it went back down
there was no frown

We had made history
and our toes were all blistery
blistery toes meant we could go
right into the flying future

The future is near, so do not fear
we will be back with a clickety-clack
flying through the air as if we have
no eyes to see what we are doing

The planes go up, for a cup
we win the prize and go back in disguise
the Wright brothers are back and
we won't leave without our sack

Medals are our pride
but now we must go and glide.
The first plane ever to fly through
bright light sky was the plane of history
and it looks so good to me!

Jamie Nichols (11)
Bottisham Village College

THE LITTLE BLUE CAR

Way back in the seventies,
a person learned to drive.
Reluctantly, reluctantly
he had to sell his car.

A few years later,
purely by chance
he saw his car
opposite his workplace

Gutted after seeing
the person who owned the car
he went back and offered more
he held his head down to the floor
and . . .

Soon he found out
that without a doubt
the car was his.
The little blue car!

Chris Wilson (12)
Bottisham Village College

MISSPELLING

People always say i get fings rong
Even if i spell it like i here it
I dident no what two fink
So i don't fink at all!

Sam Wilkinson (11)
Bretton Woods Community School

A RECIPE FOR HAPPINESS!

Take a spoonful of love
And the sweet chirping of a dove,
Add half a cup of pleasure
And a pinch of friendship . . . golden treasure!
Scoop in a teaspoon of nice,
Just to give it that extra spice
And last, but not least,
Give it a touch of delight,
Then heat it in the oven,
For your dinner tonight!
So this, my friends . . .
As you can see . . .
Is the recipe for happiness,
As good as good can be!

Sadia Henna Tariq (12)
Bretton Woods Community School

VOLCANO

The volcano blew out with anger.
With destruction in its mind.
It covered the whole town in darkness and ash.
Lava and magma flowing out like open wounds.

The lava was red-hot like coal in a fire.
Bringing down houses with ease.
Taking in trees like they were broken poles on the ground
Destruction it wanted, destruction it achieved.

Catherine Robertson (13)
Bretton Woods Community School

CLOUDS

Pure as snow, they drift endlessly;
Shapes that are formed by the wind,
By a high hill, a young man sits,
A dreamer watches the clouds
Passing through the clear blue sky.

Along the Eshi river they sail,
A small girl stares and waves,
At the dragons that keep flying without fail.

Across the heat of the desert,
Upon the sands that burn,
An outlaw with a rifle gazes
At the clouds that thirst and turn.

He knows his time is short,
In a place as harsh as this,
But the clouds will keep him company
Like a child and mother's bliss.

Gemma Sheldrake (14)
Bretton Woods Community School

MY FAMILY

My mum is a housewife
My brother goes to school
I'm in the middle,
I don't see my dad at all.

My nan is playing bingo,
My grandad's lost his job,
We're all turning crazy
Like Goldie, my pet dog!

Jessica Holland (11)
Bretton Woods Community School

THE FOX

The darkness creeps along the ground,
Silently, not making a sound.
Dusk looms nearer
The mist rises high,
The end of a day and so must sleep tight,
But not the fox, hunter of the night.

He prowls along the ground
With eyes of amber brown.
Few can detect him,
As darkness reaches its peak
The fox uses his small feet.
The fox, athlete of the night.

Quickly he draws closer with so much ease
As a fire, amongst the dead leaves.
Speed is of the essence
As he catches his prey
The fox, he sleeps,
When night drifts away.

Georgina Wilkinson (14)
Bretton Woods Community School

GHOST

On the dark, dark hill there was a
Dark, dark house and in the dark,
Dark house there was a dark, dark room,
In the dark, dark room there was a
Dark, dark cupboard, and in the dark,
Dark, cupboard there was a dark, dark box,
In the dark, dark box there was a
Ghost!

Becci Smith (11)
Bretton Woods Community School

THERE ARE TIMES

There are times

When you make me angry

Frustrated
Annoyed

There are times

When you don't seem to understand
When you don't let me do
Something I want to
When your decisions don't make sense to me

There are times when I feel

Pressurised
Trapped

Like something I'm not

There was a time

When you became ill
You lay in a hospital
I lay in my bed

Scared
Crying

I realised

You don't know how much someone means to you until
you start to lose them,
And no matter what, you are *always* right. Why?
Because you love me with all your heart
And want the best for me.

Jeanette Langford (15)
St Bede's School, Cambridge

My Grandad

His kindness shown in a smile
His old face kind and worn
Love shared between us

The meal that he cooked us when we saw him last
Made with love - we won't forget it fast

We were all so sorry that he had to go
We knew it would happen someday
But I wish I had said goodbye before he died on Sunday

A new star in my darkest night, Grandad, my universal light
When I heard my grandad was gone,
My tears came like a sad, sad song.

And now an empty hole inside of me,
The place left by my grandad's love for me

At his funeral I saw the last I'll ever see
But I sent him with this poem
A little bit of me.

'Happiness when I saw him
Fun when he tickled me
Laughter when he teased me
Warmth when he hugged me
Eagerness when he told me stories
Wonder when he showed me new things
Sad when he left me
Happiness when I remember him'.

Nathanael Dixon (12)
St Bede's School, Cambridge

SEASON SONG

First comes spring
When everything
Comes out to peep
After a very long sleep,
The sun begins to show
To melt away the winter's snow,
Uncovering lots of lovely flowers,
That I could come and watch for hours.

Summer is next in line,
When the weather is fine,
Everything is warm and bright,
There isn't a cloud in sight.
It's blistering hot,
The wind is not
Blowing at all,
And the flowers grow tall.

Autumn is always very mellow,
When the leaves begin to turn yellow
And they fall from the trees,
At the slightest breeze.
Hanging onto the branches, like delicate petals,
The grass glistens like lots of metals.

Winter comes last,
When the wind begins to blow
And there is a hint of snow,
There is a chill in the air,
The branches are all bare.

Sophie Pearson (12)
St Bede's School, Cambridge

THE UNCERTAINTY OF YOUTH

I hold the future in my hands
Its form is constantly changing.
Sometimes it's calm -
I can control it.
But then it's wild and ragged
A jumbled mess I'm not able to manage.
It shivers when it's nervous:
Grows bigger when it's hopeful.
Sometimes it completely disappears
And I don't know where to search for it.
You hold the past in your hands.
Aged and full of wisdom,
Yet bigger and fresher than ever.
Steady. Glowing with comfort
Like a lantern in the mist.
Bold with success.
Casually it seeps through
To join in conversations.
Mellow, subtle, calming.
It eases the future I hold,
To let it rest in the knowledge
That really,
It will be alright.

Louise Pigott (16)
St Bede's School, Cambridge

DOLPHINS AND OCEAN

The waves dancing and galloping around,
Dolphins leaping out of the ocean,
The waves crash together with a ferocious sound,
The dolphins move with a graceful motion!

Sparkling, glistening, the waves skip and run,
Glistening, sparkling, racing, tranquillity,
The prancing ocean water catches the sun,
Away from the roaring crowds of the city!

Emily Lygo (12)
St Bede's School, Cambridge

LOST FREEDOM

Darkness, damp and decay rule that lonely home,
Still the old man lives there, all alone.
As ancient as the bricks within the wall.
He waits, hoping somebody will call.
All day, every day, he sits there still
He knows nobody ever will.
At the window, he gazes out.
He constantly watches everything about.
He stares resentfully at the children playing.
He listens intently to what they are saying.
Always reflecting upon the thoughts in his head,
Forever wishing he was outside instead.
When he was a young boy, he was happy, full of joy.
He used to run, to laugh and to have fun.
He had a loving family and lived without a care.
Back then when sad moments were only very rare.
He had friends by the score
And everyone's house was an open door.
All those years ago, he could not possibly want more.
Now memories are all he does hold,
He treasures them as though they are gold.
Sitting in his living room, he is full of gloom.
Again he looks at the children, with resent,
For his lost freedom they represent.

Rachel Lister (15)
St Bede's School, Cambridge

MY PETS

I have two guinea pigs,
Called Honey and Daisy.
Daisy is so lazy,
And Honey is so funny.
Honey is a tan colour,
Daisy is all black.
I sit and watch them
Racing around the run.
They have so much fun,
Running in and out of tubes,
And munching on their food.
Tomato, carrot and cucumber
Are their favourites, as well
As plenty of dried food and hay.
They seem to want to munch all day.
They like to squeak and chatter.
They like a good old natter.
At night I shut them in their hutch,
So they don't get up to much.
I say 'Goodnight, sleep tight.'

Gemma Thomas (11)
St Bede's School, Cambridge

MAN AND ME

He lies upon a hospital bed,
With tubes and wires about his head,
And me with energy to spare
And feeling wrong, should I be there?

An independent, forthright man,
Him brave, experienced, more than I.
While me with life, so always there.
No life in old age - *is it fair?*

Now I have life, I'm ready to know,
What can I do to let him go?
His brain is sharp; his strength has gone.
For him, his life, just lingers on.

Oliver Worth (15)
St Bede's School, Cambridge

THE SUN

The sun, the sun blazing in the sky
The sun, the sun, yellow and red with its beautiful rays.
Some day we can't help but see his wonderful glazes.
The sun, the sun, floating in the sky
When the sun goes down, the sky, it dies.
But when it comes up, the sky is filled
With lovely colours, you'll be thrilled.
But when it rains, the sky turns black,
The clouds turn grey and then the sun goes away.

The sun, the sun, sparkles like glitter,
Whatever the day, whatever the weather.
The seasons of the year are all filled with sun,
But not all of them are filled with warmth and fun!
Winter is cold with a bit of light.
Autumn is when the trees' leaves fall to the ground.
And they are the colour of the sun.

Spring is sun with freshness, the sun, it makes everything grow,
And summer is fun with sun and the seaside.
The sun is as hot as boiling water,
And some days it decides when to shine on everyone,
But when the sun goes, the moon comes with the night.

Louise Deane (11)
St Bede's School, Cambridge

FOUR LEGS, TWO EYES AND A TAIL

Chewing, shredding, clawing at a toy.
Snarling, biting, tearing at each other's throats.
That's a puppy's life.

Eating, drinking, gulping from a bowl.
Curling, yawning, settling down for the night in a tiny home.
That's a puppy's life.

'Sit!' 'Come!' Collar's put around your neck.
Stroking, petting, tall figures bending down to pick you up.
That's a puppy's life.

Lead on, walking around the garden.
Sniffing things, chewing things, exploring. Back inside to safety.
That's a puppy's life.

Going outside, poking your head through the pen walls.
Staring through the barriers and sniffing strange smells.
I wonder what the real world's like?

Michael Stone (15)
St Bede's School, Cambridge

FRIENDS

When you cry, I'll wipe your tears
When you're scared, I'll take your fears
When you're low, I'll give you hope
When you're alone, I'll help you cope
When you're sleeping, I'll wish you a sweet dream

When your heart beats I'll be with you and never let you go.
When you're with me, I'll be so, so *happy!*

Annalisa Dichello (11)
St Bede's School, Cambridge

WAR

What is it good for?
Who knows?
It tears countries apart.
It makes neighbours and friends enemies
And it costs billions.
A waste
Of young men and lives.
They leave full of dreams, of glory and fame.
They return horrified, never the same.
Some with injuries, blown-off limbs and suchlike.
Some never return.
How can that be good or right?
War!
What is it good for?

Jeremy Badley (13)
St Bede's School, Cambridge

SIAN

She cuts through the air,
like a knife cutting through butter.
Her eyes scan over the land,
like a telescope to the sky.
She glides from her perch to grab
her prey in her needle-sharp talons.
When it starts to get dark
she'll sit on her perch with her head
tucked under her wing and that's
how she'll stay until the next day begins.

Carmine Ruggièro (11)
St Bede's School, Cambridge

MEN

Just look at men today - they're not what we need!
They're all dogs . . . I'm not going near one without a lead!
'No, honestly, babe, you don't need *my* number - *I'll* call *you!*'
Don't believe it girls, all lies; nothing they say is true!
Pathetic panting, whimpering dogs: pleading to be fussed -
Don't give in ladies - there isn't even *one* you can trust!
Look at them strutting, thinking they're so 'cool'!
If you think you can train them, you're a fool!
Honestly, you'd think we'd learn to leave them well alone
But we beg and plead, and fall at their feet - it would be easier
                                        to buy them a bone!
If you see one wandering, don't keep what you've found;
Trust your instincts, girls and take him to the pound!
However, it isn't *all* bad - some men come in handy . . .
Like for making others jealous of your hunk of eye candy!

Becky Wright (15)
St Bede's School, Cambridge

RUGBY

He fell in the mud
With a terrible thud.
The ball whizzed past
Ever so fast.
He thought he saw stars
And life on Mars,
But when he got up
His team had the cup
And the game was
                    over!

Sam Bolton (11)
St Bede's School, Cambridge

FRODO'S LAMENT

My burden grows heavy,
Here on my chest.
My heart is weary,
I can find no rest.

My eyes grow tired,
My body cold.
My strength starts to fade,
My soul feels old.

My will wears weak,
My courage frail.
But all is not lost,
Until we should fail.

So still I do struggle,
Through the dust and the gloom,
To destroy the One Ring,
In the fires of Mount Doom.

Ben Thompson (13)
St Bede's School, Cambridge

THE WONDERFUL PLACE

There is a place, a wondrous place
Which all men desire to find,
This Nirvana or Heaven's gate
A hidden niche conclave,
Perhaps a piece of mind,
There is a place not in my head
I have found it in my dreams
Of course it is my bed!

James Boyle (12)
St Bede's School, Cambridge

THE ZOO

Stripy, spotty
and even dotty,
these are the animals of the zoo

The lions roar
and the eagles soar
into the silent starry sky

Crocodiles bask in the midday sun
whilst playful monkeys are having fun
like children on the swings and slides

Zebras' fur all black and white
snakes with skins that fit so tight
like the ladies' fishnet stockings

Seals slide to catch the fish
almost like a tasty wish
feeding time is here again

Flamingos stand on a single leg
whilst wolves sit up and beg
as a poor person waits for something to eat

The panda eats his bamboo sticks
the kangaroo doesn't want to mix
with the animals living there.

The gigantic giraffes stride around
the elephant makes a trumpeting sound
louder than a big brass band

The hungry bats flap and screech
while the lemur eats a ripe peach
why are they looking at me?

Parrots chatter to each other
whilst the cubs play near their mother
in the den in the zoo.

Hannah Brown (11)
St Bede's School, Cambridge

CHRISTMAS DAY

Sitting up in my room,
Time to open presents soon,
Mum and Dad still snoring loud,
Fluffy purring, strong and proud!

Sitting here, expectations high,
Minutes passing slowly by,
Eight o'clock, eight-fifteen,
Want to see if Santa's been!

Hearing footsteps hit the floor,
Hear a knocking at my door,
I leg it fast by my mum,
Finally the time has come!

I really can't believe my very eyes,
Presents; different shape and size,
Big, small, round, tall,
I really think Christmas is cool!

Angelina Sabatino (12)
St Bede's School, Cambridge

PAS DE CHARGE

Great round shot and shell do pummel his lines most relentlessy.
Again and again do these bronze cannons belch mighty
plumes of smoke, channelling their wrath against him.
The steel-tipped Forrest advances upon him to the roar or
'Vive l'Empereur'.
Yet still he does not break.
Commit the Imperial Guard,
I will not.

The guns grow hotter and the gunners do toil to plague him
with splinter and shard.
The drums are fainter now as they echo about the walls of
La Haye Sainte.
The farmstead-turned-battlement is now a cavern of
slaughter and screams.
His line seems to falter, red-clad men begin to leave the ridge.
Is he soon to break?
Commit the Imperial Guard,
I will not.

Marshal Ney advances, five thousand flamboyantly-attired
but grim-faced cavalry do flank him like some great rippling cloak.
The horses do trot, then gallop and finally charge,
The capture of the ridge, their only goal.
Bugles screech out and cut across the air, the sky begins to darken,
The sabre-edged wave floods over the crest and is
enveloped in smoke as the muskets crack out.
Horse and rider fall, colours and eagles topple,
the flood is halted and swiftly turned.
Falter he does not
Commit the Imperial Guard,
I will

March forward they do, a sheer wall of bayonets
and bearskins.
Ney does return blade broken
and bloody.

His part has been played but the tragedy must run to its end.
The Old Guard assail the slope and it is now he appears
The Iron Duke canters forth to win the day.
I see an anvil made from British squares and the hammer
appears in the form of Prussian columns.
The order to fire is given and the Guard fall by the drove,
they waver and then finally break.
Pursued by the Reds' horses they flee.

The day is lost and the army spent.
Napoleon is beaten and his beloved Old Guard
smashed upon the rocks.

Chris Chapman (15)
St Bede's School, Cambridge

THE DRAGON

His nose blew out fire like a Bunsen
His eyes gleamed like pearls
His mouth dripped blood
He smiled. A deadly smile.

The sky was black like coal
His body shone out like stars at night
Pure beauty. Yet pure evil his body read,
His scaly body rippled like water when it's windy

Lightning flashed across the evening sky,
His body stood out for a minute as he took off
His enormous bulk flew gracefully
He roared! Sending shivers down Death's back.

The dragon had awoken.

Mark Slade (12)
St Bede's School, Cambridge

MY REASON FOR LIVING

I woke up this morning, despaired where I lay
A new chance for torment, a whole brand new day
Pulled a comb through my bedhead, clumped down the stairs
Greeted by anger, criticism my breakfast
Fought my battles, came in last.

Then school; a milling scream of students
I hid; retreated to that secret place so calm and still inside my head
Lived a lifetime in my dreams.
'You've forgotten your homework.'
Blink in surprise; I had homework?
'Sorry Miss, I went away.'

Come evening, I lie on my bed
Bruised pride, sore head
Skewered with hurt, a human pincushion
Wanting to cry, wishing to die.

But then there's you.

Your sweet, caring tone,
The lingering looks when we're all alone
The letters you write me,
Magical letters that can summon a smile or banish my doubts
The feel of your arm slung casually over my shoulders, holding
                                            me together
Sometimes I feel I will shatter like glass, millions of
                                sharp hurting pieces
But then there's you, neutralising my warring pains with your affection.

Please never leave me, never go away
Be mine always, forever stay
I know I love you, my tower of strength,
Through the bad and the good, be there few
My reason for living
If you but knew.

Rachel Moseley (15)
St Bede's School, Cambridge

COMPUTERS

There's a bleep, bleep . . .
Hummmmm, the screen jumps into life.
Colours flashing on and off,
Words coming up too fast to read.

Fidgeting, hurrying, shaking the mouse.
The computer is humming, thinking.
Double-click on Explorer,
Time to explore the World Wide Web.

Banging the keyboard in frustration,
Bright colours appear and flash.
My favourite site appears,
Password? Done, okay, hurry up!

A whole new world has opened,
Like a huge treasure box
Filled with facts, fiction, games and more,
Waiting to be explored.

Claire Scofield (12)
St Bede's School, Cambridge

RABBIT

Inside the rabbit's teeth, the soft nibble.
Inside the soft nibble, the rabbit's claw.
Inside the rabbit's claw, the nasty scratch.
Inside the nasty scratch, the drop of blood.
Inside the drop of blood, the rabbit's water.
Inside the rabbit's water, the rabbit's foot.
Inside the rabbit's foot, the five claws.
Inside the five claws, the sudden hop.
Inside the sudden hop, the glinting eyes.
Inside the glinting eyes, the rabbit's teeth.

Maisie Rowsell (12)
St Bede's School, Cambridge

FIREWORKS AND BONFIRES

Fizzling fireworks fly up high,
Swishing and swirling in the sky.
Bonfire burning, hot and bright,
Lighting up the sky at night.

Sparklers glowing for a while,
Fireworks seen as far as a mile.
Fireworks shooting very high,
While children look at the guy.

Lucy Fussinger-Coles (12)
St Bede's School, Cambridge

AUTUMN

As I walk through the park,
Autumn is here.
The leaves starting to turn
Green, yellow and rich rusty reds.
Bare and empty branches all around.
Carpets of leaves rustle beneath my feet
Soft, gentle sounds of animals in the distance.
Clear blue skies like the glistening of a sea.
A shiver deep down inside.
Signs of winter coming.
Dark and cold days just around the corner.
Time to go home around the log fire.

Brett Holloway
St Bede's School, Cambridge

THE BOMBING

Crashing, burning, rage of fire.
screams, cries, shouts.
The darkness of night, broken by
the dancing of crackling flames,
the quiet of the city pierced by
sirens, buildings collapsing.
Confusion's rippling body races
through the city,
moans of the dying.
Death and destruction are all that remain.

Sarah Thompson (13)
St Bede's School, Cambridge

SOLAR SYSTEM

All nine planets
Circle our sun
Nearest is Mercury
Furthest is Pluto

Mars looks so angry
As the surface shines red
Jupiter is the biggest
With gravity so strong

Stars shine brightly in our Milky Way
This is our galaxy where we belong

Earth is our planet, all blue and clean
Our world has one moon
That glows in the night

The sun shines proudly
Lighting up the sky
Some days it's hot
Some days it's not

The sun gives us life
On this planet so blue
We now live in space
And land on the moon

What is that star
So small and so bright?
Could it be Venus
That glows in the night?
Could it be Saturn with large golden rings?

Our rockets will travel to Neptune and back
Us humans may go to faraway homes
Look back at our planet with wide open eyes
Aren't we so lucky to be part of this world?

Christopher Thurston (12)
St Bede's School, Cambridge

THE WORLD WITHIN

Camera poised,
Ready to capture, enclose and parcel up
The hidden world
That I cannot quite grasp
In this ethereal light.
Water gushes behind me
And yet the water does not move and
My tranquil world makes no sound.
Moss star sprinkles
Poke their four-petaled heads
Out from below the
Crumpled rippling grass carpet.
The smell of freshness floats on air
And the wild blossom water honey
Sweeping through the journey's lifeline,
Brings me back.
The camera is still poised
And I have captured the hidden world,
But not on my photo -
It dwells in my head, comforting,
To be revisited at any time.

Rosie Martin (14)
St Bede's School, Cambridge

THAT IS THE JOY OF THE FESTIVAL

A noisy street filled with people,
Balloons hang high from a church steeple,
Luminous lights and lanterns hang high,
Fireworks erupt in the dark night sky,
That is the joy of the festival.

Dancing divas dance the night away,
To the beat of the music bodies sway,
Speedily spinning, jiving, bopping,
Hoping the music won't be stopping,
That is the joy of the festival.

Everyone's happy, having fun,
Children playing, joyfully run,
Playing games, eagerly eating,
Drinking too much, the fizzy's repeating,
That is the joy of the festival.

Crowd around for the fancy dress parade,
A girl dressed up as a servant maid,
Boys dressed up as Peter Pan,
Over there is an Elvis Presley fan,
That is the joy of the festival.

Cymbals crashing like broken glass,
Orchestras of woodwind and of brass,
Gospel choirs sing God's word,
All this music, for miles is heard,
That is the joy of the festival.

Litter lies there throughout the street,
Injured people are given a seat,
Children lost scream for their mum,
Drunken people on the road with bottles of rum,
All this for the joy of the festival.

Bethan Walker (12)
St Bede's School, Cambridge

MY CANARIES

My canaries live
at my grandad's house.
They make a lot of noise
not quiet like a mouse.
The twittering and whistling
of those little birds
it makes such a racket
that it gets on my nerves.
They eat lots of birdseed
and little bits of fruit.
They lay little blue eggs,
the babies are really cute.
Grandad cleans out the cages
and washes them out.
If he doesn't do it
then Nana will shout.
He makes lots of cages
and sells them at shows.
He's won lots of prizes.
How many? Who knows?
In summer the birds
lose feathers all round.
They blow up in the breezes
then land on the ground.
The new ones are wonderful
orange, yellow and red
and some are all white.
Yes, even their heads.
Cats, dogs and hamsters
all things that are hairy,
are just not a patch on
my brilliant canaries!

Sam Challis (11)
St Bede's School, Cambridge

How It Used To Be

'Back in my day' my father always used to say,
Well, it's my day now and I want to change the world somehow.
I'm going to be radical; make a difference,
Not like everyone else, make my life have some significance.

Everyone makes mistakes,
I bet you did when you were young.
I want to rebel, live wild and break free,
Turn away from what my life used to be.

'When I was young' well, I am young and innocent,
Don't try to protect me; you'll push me away,
Please honour my judgement of friends - I would do
But believe me, I also need you.

'What no Latin, no more beatings in school?
What is the world coming to these days,'* my father says.
Well, choices, opinions and freedom of speech,
That's what they always teach.

Why are you worrying? I'm not interested in sex, drugs
                                    and rock 'n' roll,
Please don't hold me back; you'll only look like a fool!
Don't place your past mistakes on me,
I'm not you, and I don't want to be.

'It's not like the good old days.'
Time moves on and so should you,
I want to look back on my schooldays and the craze,
With fondness, and to let my children enjoy them too.

Dad, please let me go,
Find out about life, before I fly away and cut you like a knife.
You won't lose me; so there's no need to feel low,
Thank you for your guidance and all that you've shown.

I'm growing up now, and having a ball,
Please . . . just let me be me, that's who I am after all!

Lydia Titmus (15)
St Bede's School, Cambridge

IF I COULD CHANGE THE WORLD

If I could change the world, there'd be no such thing as guilt
because in my world there'd be nothing to be guilty of!

If I could change the world we'd have no guns to fight,
we'd walk down dark alleys without a second thought.

If I could change the world, no one would know how to hurt,
the world would be full of smiles - the way things are meant to be.

But I can't change the world just like that, these changes
need many years,
But I can start with me and make a small difference now!

I'll be as good as gold and bear no guilt.
I'll never use a weapon to hurt, whether it's a gun or unkind words.

I'll smile all day, I'll make others smile as well.
If only everyone did this, the world could be paradise.

So change yourself today, it's not that hard to do.
Just wear a smile, think before you act and we can all make a
difference today.

Olivia Pinnock (12)
St Bede's School, Cambridge

LEFT

She left,
Didn't say a word,
Just left,
I didn't hear her leave,
When will she return?
She left nothing for me to remember her by,
Just left,
Didn't say a word.
Her clothes still hang in the wardrobe,
Her shoes all neatly stacked,
Her bed is made and her curtains are shut,
The room is like a museum,
Her museum, her life, her memories.
She's left,
Left me to go through life alone,
Worried, confused,
She left,
Why?
Did I do something?
Why cause all of this pain?
I need you, you're my sister,
I look to you for advice, guidance,
You've left,
Left me,
Left us alone.
Such pain,
Such confusion.
Such love, lost,
You've left.

Jenny Warnes (15)
St Bede's School, Cambridge

SEASONS

Lovely spring
When all things are new
Trees blossoming
And animals arriving

These are the seasons
The wonderful seasons

Sunny summer
As it comes
The hot sun is happiness
When people are swimming in the pools.

These are the seasons
The wonderful seasons

Awesome autumn
Leaves like a blanket over the ground
The wind goes *whooo*
At the end

These are the seasons
The wonderful seasons

Cold winter
Everywhere is covered in snow
The iced puddles are like people's eyes
When it is lovely Christmas or even New Year

These are the seasons
The wonderful seasons.

Jacqueline Allum (12)
St Bede's School, Cambridge

YOUTH VS THE WORLD

It's us versus them
The savage beast against the gentle creature
They make the rules
We live by them

And we're tired of living with them

Our limitations are limitless
They are in complete control
No drink, no self-control
No respect, no fun

No life

After years of it the teens are starting to revolt
Slowly the savage world is being overrun
And youth is taking over
The respect for the rules no longer exists

Now the time has come

Powered through the lyrics of self-righteous music
The world is being plunged headlong into a new age
An age not powered by the rules
An age when everyone's opinion is valued

An age where teens have a right to some fun

But when I look around I don't like what I see
On the surface it's fun
But on the inside it's a completely different story

I enjoy this way of life as much as the next person does
But some people just take it too far

This lawless society is starting to have an effect
On the people who control it

The number of teen suicides is increasing every year
As does the availability of drugs
These drugs having a bad effect on the teens
And the world is turning into a dark and violent place

It's barely safe to walk the streets

Is this really the world we want to live in?

Richard Griffiths (15)
St Bede's School, Cambridge

WAR

Bullets flew over my head,
As I slept in my trench bed.
A rattling of guns in the sky,
As I crawled by.

Then a grenade did glide through the air,
It was as big as a pear.
I ran away as quick as a hare,
As the bomb exploded in scorching flames.
Not at all stopped by the rain.

A roaring noise behind me
I turned and saw a tank rolling forward
The rattling of guns stopped.
I saw the enemy fleeing
And our army cheering.

Steven Kylstra (12)
St Bede's School, Cambridge

THE CIRCUS

The circus is here, my mate said,
That'll get us out of going early to bed,

I think we should ask if we can go,
I hope they say yes then we can see the show,

Hot dogs and candyfloss, there's lots to eat,
Look at that clown, he's got big feet,

Going into the Big Top, our hearts beat faster,
Who's over there? It must be the ringmaster,

The lights are flashing, the music pumping,
Out into the ring come little dogs jumping,

Next come the jugglers with their batons flying,
Perhaps we could do that tomorrow, we'll be trying,

We all look up to see the trapeze artists swinging,
Oh, what's that noise? My mobile phone is ringing,

Let's go and get something to eat and drink,
After the break it the clowns and skateboarders I think,

The clowns are really funny, the skateboarders too,
Help! Does anybody know the way to the loo?

We do lots of clapping and our hands are sore,
Then everyone is rushing to get to the door!

Toby Matthew Dainton
St Bede's School, Cambridge

56

THE BATTLE OF THE AIR

Dawn awakes
Another new day expecting rivalry in the air
Pilots casually lean against sheds and hangars
And in the CO's hut the phone rings, 'Squadron scramble!'
Pilots sprint to their machines getting in
'Chocks away!' the pilots call, forward go the throttles
And the aircraft go lumbering forward, like angry beasts
Up they thunder to intercept and then the commotion starts
Leaders call demanding positions, Ops Room getting vicious
Then in the distance a line appears - the opposition
Screaming fighters with roaring bombers
Tracers fill the air as pilots call to each other
Teeth chattering, guns chattering, flinching when your aircraft shudders
Checking over your shoulder to see if anyone is there
Looking around to see if your friends are there
Then you see your chance, a lone aircraft
You go after it
Eyes marking it
Pull the trigger!
Guns flashing
Bullets thrashing
Suddenly the aircraft in front starts to shake
Engine howling
Ripping cowling
Flames burst everywhere
Then the pilot jumps out to safety - hope his parachute comes out
Maybe . . .

Michael Hooper (12)
St Bede's School, Cambridge

ALL ABOUT ME

I like playing football
Kicking up against the wall
It's better than school
Which is not really cool.

I like chips and beans
Chocolate, by any means
Wearing my old jeans
And I like to watch TV
Just my mother and me,
Sitting on the settee
With a nice cup of tea.

Playing in the park
Fireworks after dark
Out with Johnny Mark
And just having a lark.

I like going to Scouts
Especially when we're out
At camp or on a hike
And I love riding my bike.

I don't like going to Norwich
Snails, homework, or cold porridge,
I don't like being in pain
Or getting caught in the rain.

I don't like feeling sad
Or people when they're bad
Or when I get into a fight
With my brother every night.

So now we're at the end
Of my little poem, my friend,
I think that you now see
This is what makes me me!

Andrew Trocian (11)
St Bede's School, Cambridge

I HATE YOU

'I hate you,' he spat into
The air as he
Turned and stomped away.
The habitual feeling engulfed
Him with it's comforting
Familiarity,
But this time,
Threatening to overtake him,
Hate, festering.
Turning him into a new being
Tearing away at him
Taunting him to
Hurt,
Destroy,
But he could not
Recognise that hate turns,
Turns in on itself
And instead of destroying,
Those he hated
It had
Already
Virtually
Destroyed
Him.

Reuben Mashford (15)
St Bede's School, Cambridge

LAST WEEK'S KID . . .

Where I live there's no such thing as friends,
We're all in groups, following trends.
We're out of school; we're out at night,
This morning we'll play, later we'll fight.

In my group, you're in or you're out,
I think I'm in, well just about.
Unlike that poor kid from last week,
His future is definitely bleak.

I don't want to be part of this,
But I know I'm in and can't be dismissed.
I may not have a first-class honours degree,
But this is wrong and I wish they could see.

I try to stop them: 'It's not worth his life!'
But I'm not the one carrying the knife.
They know I'm weak and I'm unsure,
That's why my role is nothing more:

I take all their blame,
And I stand in their shame.
But I'm not stupid and even without my honours degree,
I can see where this role will land me:

'It's not worth his life!'

It's worth mine.

Elizabeth Cameron (15)
St Bede's School, Cambridge

WHY ME?

It gets harder and harder each day for me
Walking to school, hoping they're not there,
I can see them laughing and shouting
But all I can do is stand and stare,
They make my life a misery at school
Kicking me and making me cry,
I go home every day and tell my mum everything is fine
But then go to my room and wish they would die,
They say in all magazines that bullies are cowards
But I'm the one that's scared to go to school,
They say you should tell a teacher
But if I do they would do something mean and cruel,
When will it end?
Over and finished like a nightmare,
Bad dream or reality
Too close to even compare,
They steal my dinner money
Spending it on drugs and fags,
The girls they hang about with are worse,
Tarts and dirty slags,
No one notices I'm hurting inside
Breaking apart,
Like a school romance ending
With the tears and the broken hearts,
I tried praying to God
Asking Him now much longer?
If I'm going to finish dead
Or if I'm going to get stronger?
They've ruined my chances of being who I want to be
The only thing I can say to them is
Why me?

Sarah Nightingale (16)
St Bede's School, Cambridge

RISE AND FALL . . .

As a child I had every mission patch,
From Mercury to Apollo,
From my rickety wooden lunar module,
Perched among the branches in my backyard
I orbited the Earth with John Glenn,
And was first around the moon with Borman, Lovell and Anders.

Each night I gazed at the stars through the hatch window,
And each day I pondered the sensation of bounding across the moon.
I was part of a time of golden achievements,
An unforgettable patriotic masterpiece.

The world held its breath for the USA.

In 1966, Daddy had gone on holiday to Vietnam,
Mummy said we needed a smaller house.
So we changed our trajectory to Brooklyn.
On the 32nd floor there were no backyards.
I mourned the loss of my lunar module, *Manifest Destiny.*

In 1969 Neil Armstrong finally stood,
Where I had stood a thousand times before.
But for the first time in the history of manned missions,
I did not step out with him,
I did not stand beside Gene Kranz in Mission Control,
I did not sit beside Mike Collins orbiting the moon.

I sat and watched two lone men,
Step on a distant planet,
240,000 statute miles away.

Later I stood in the concrete stairwell
And stared as I had done many times before up at the moon,

But this time was the first time I noticed how very far away it was.

Rebecca Clarke (15)
St Bede's School, Cambridge

THE DARE

The bottle spun, it pointed in her direction
'Truth or dare?'
Giggles surrounded, as whispers streamed
Anxiety filled her body

Confusion flowed as the words came
'We dare you . . .'
The beating got faster and faster
No turning back

Her body shook with nerves
'You can't be serious?'
Mixed emotions stormed through her head
'Thump, thump, thump'

She leaned over her best friend
'Ready?'
Lips pressed together, stuck fast like superglue
Eyes shone around the room, fascination and wonder-filled

Her spine tingled as their tongues caressed
'Two girls? That's twisted'
It felt like it lasted a lifetime
Excitement flooded her body mixed with confusion

Both girls' hearts raced as they pulled away
'I never knew it could feel like that'
Anticipation pumped through their veins
Like a child on Christmas Eve

As her hand caressed her thigh, it happened again
'Isn't this wrong?'
Passion submerged through them.
'Truth or dare?'

Claire Osbourn (15)
St Bede's School, Cambridge

TRIALS AND TRIBULATIONS

It's my life; it's my life please,
Keep out, keep out of my life.
It's time to go, it's time to go,
Go to school, I must go now.

I go to school to catch the bus,
I cannot go without a fuss,
I must go now or I'll be late,
I forgot my books so I am in a state.

I catch the bus to go to school,
The driver is mad at us all.
He's in a hurry and not very funny,
We are going to be late, oh, what a state!

We arrive at school and go straight to the hall,
To find the teachers having a ball.
It's time to teach, it's time to teach the teachers
Weep, as it's time to teach.

Oh, what time is it now? Oh, what time
Is it now? It is time to go, well I do
Not know if it is time to go, oh, I hope so.

I get back on the bus this time
Without a fuss.
The driver is happy the end is near
We all want to go home and that is clear.
We arrive at my stop and I get off with a hop.
I run home to my house as quiet as a mouse.
I bang on the door saying, 'I will not go there anymore.'

Stephen Waine (11)
St Bede's School, Cambridge

CONSOLES

Slowly as you push the little red button,
the screen turns on with pictures
coming from channels available.
The clicking sound you can hear,
once you have pushed the button which turns it on.
The colours slowly start to look funny as you play hour after hour,
                                                          after hour.
The screen looks weird and fuzzy during your first hour of play.
The television slowly brings you to it and you can, or will easily get
                                                          addicted to this.
It walks you to it then you get trapped in it.
Play or pay, it's my way now, I decide, I do what I tell it to.
Like television, but this time it's in for a real chance.
My brother, 9, downstairs watching TV and I can hear it so
I turn the volume higher on mine.
I have not turned the light on yet, because I like the darkness,
It makes me feel like I've more control.
It might brainwash me to play but at least I complete the level.
I get rammed into the pit of doom,
And the TV looks like it has taken over me.
I try to get out but it has me trapped inside its portal of doom.
It gets the controller and starts to chase me, I'm in the game now.
The big monster in the game starts to chase me and this might
                                                          be the end.
After, I just wake up and find out it was just a dream.
The sounds made it sound real.
It could happen to you, so be careful what you play!

Al-Nahyan Mubarak (11)
St Bede's School, Cambridge

LATE!

Got up this morning
Bed called,
'Get back in here!'
'Can't,' I said, 'late.'

Went downstairs
Opened the fridge
Then shut it.
Fridge called 'Open me!'
'Can't,' I said, 'late.'

Walked past the car
It said, 'Get in here!'
'Can't,' I said, 'late.'

Got to work
My boss said,
'Can I see you in my office?'
'Can't,' I said, 'late.'

Sat down at my desk
The secretary said,
'Would you like a coffee?'
'Can't,' I said, 'late.'

Phone rang, it said
'Pick me up!'
'Can't,' I said, 'late.'

'Office is closing for tonight.'
'Let me stay a bit longer.'
'Okay but remember to close.'
'Can't,' I said, 'late.'

Tom MacQueen (11)
St Bede's School, Cambridge

YOU SAID YOU'D BE THERE

You said you'd always be there for me
You said you really cared
You left, I didn't know what to do
Why did you leave me?
You said you'd be there.

I really, really needed you
You said you'd help me through
I had no one else to turn to
Where else could I have gone?
You said you'd be there.

I was so happy when you were here.
Now I'm so sad that you've left me alone
I thought you really cared for me
But where were you when I needed you?
You said you'd be there.

I thought we'd stay together forever
I thought you'd always be by my side.
I'm lost now that you've left me
Did I do something wrong?
You said you'd always be there.

Stephanie Allum (16)
St Bede's School, Cambridge

WAR

War creeps up to his victim leaving a trail of blood behind.
War creeps up to his victim giving it a present of death.
War kills a body every second
War makes the Earth a hostile place.
War choking up the Earth.

Joshua James Drury (11)
St Bede's School, Cambridge

THE SEMI-FINALS

Kick it off,
Throw it in,
See where it will go,
When it hits the ground
Give it a little kick
And up the pitch it will go.
To a forward,
Then a back and a centre and
Yessss!
It's a goal!
The crowd goes wild!
All we hear is
'Hooray, hooray, we're off to the finals!
But then the other team scores.
Oh no!
What's happening?
The ref has disallowed it.
'We've won, hooray!'
The crowds are running wild, up and down the street.
They shout 'We're going to the finals, we can't wait,
It's going to be great!'

The streets go quiet as they all go to bed,
Tired and smiling with glee.
For tomorrow is the *final,*
Which they hope to win.

Naomi Collen (12)
St Bede's School, Cambridge

HALLOWE'EN

Hallowe'en is finally here,
Out the window I do peer.
Seeing ghouls and ghosts run by,
Scaring people like you and I.

The doorbell rings,
The monster sings.
My brother's scared,
The sweets are shared.

I see a witch come up the path
Practising her cackling laugh
I open the door and she says, 'Trick or treat?'
So I hand over my very last sweet.

Hallowe'en is now over
And I'm going to bed.
This long day has
            gone to my head.

Jamie Whitlock (12)
St Bede's School, Cambridge

HORSES CANTER

His precious velvet parted lips,
bold and young.
Her eyes gazed with savage power,
as a force of horses coming together.
Her calm blue eye streaked his cheek,
intrigued and excited, they walked
in circles, side to side.
Set into a canter!

Alice Myers (14)
St Mary's School, Cambridge

MEANINGFUL LIFE

As an orange, I am round and fleshy;
Blaze of sunlight hits on my skin and it is reflected.
My master walks towards me,
Picks me up and inspects me;
I feel dizzy as he turns me around
But I glint in the light like the sun.
I am not staying any longer.
He gently pricks his cold, shiny knife into me,
Then starts crafting his mighty masterpiece.
As the harsh, sharpened knife gets deeper into me,
I cry aloud in pain.
An outlet of tears and blood
Splash on my master and scatter on the ground;
My skin is shredded bit by bit.
The soreness finally stings into my heart,
Seeing my body being sliced open, segment by segment;
Though, it is not the end of my life.
My soul wafts in the air,
Giving out lives and health;
And in my master's body where I live,
Forever and ever!

Yu Ting Chau (15)
St Mary's School, Cambridge

NIGHTS UNTOLD

The deep night stirred,
Powerless dreams were shaken.
Spiritually bruised, he stood stall.
The quarters shone whiter than ever,
Long, gold coins tapped in his pocket,
A queer silence hung softly.

Ayomide Sule (14)
St Mary's School, Cambridge

THE NOISES OF THE WORLD

Two chairs begin to squeak in turn
Like two mice discussing the day.
Distant pens scratch and scrape on paper
Like a cat scraping desperately at a bedroom door.
A thump of a giant's footsteps
Walking briskly along the corridor.
The tip-tap of builders tap-dancing.
The trees softly whispering together
About when there will next be rain.
A violin player playing discreetly to himself
But imagining a whole orchestra behind him.
The drone of the lights gently humming
Like a piano playing a flat note forever.
Suddenly a loud cough enters the air
Like a sudden blast from an opposing side.

Emily Bradley (13)
St Mary's School, Cambridge

MUSICAL SILENCE

I hear the determined silence of thought,
I hear brains working like clockwork,
I hear the leaves that whisper in the wind,
I hear the birdsong whistle through the sky,
I hear the monotonous drone of electrical lighting,
I hear an explosive cough like a blast from a cannon,
I hear the low buzz of far-off chatter,
I hear the chairs squeaking like trees in the breeze,
As I sit here in the classroom
I hear the silence of the world.

Sophie Brown (13)
St Mary's School, Cambridge

HERE ONE MINUTE, GONE THE NEXT

The stranger inspects his quest,
As the waxy innocent fruit gleams in the light.
He draws back his weapon and stabs the flesh,
As if a pin were popping a balloon,
The orange cries, whilst the fruity tears slide along his bony fingers.
He crafts away, hacking at the rind,
The cold metal simply being guided by his master,
Slow, clean cuts as he works towards the pleasure awaiting him.
One by one, he reveals the succulent segments,
A single gulp destroys each crescent-like piece.
As the zesty smell wafts through the stale air,
Mouths throughout the room water in jealousy.
The end draws near as he wipes his slate clean.

Suzannah Charlotte Munday (15)
St Mary's School, Cambridge

THE BEAST

As I sit in the shallows of the room, I watch a beast,
His eyes caress the curves of his victim.
He picks up a sharpened knife and plunges it into the mysterious object.
The object gives out a weak cry as its rich juice is released.
The beast gradually dissects his prize, with a blank expression,
He is not ashamed of his actions.
As the flesh of the innocent victim is revealed, the fresh zest
                                        lightens the air.
When the beast comes to the end of his masterpiece he slowly
                                        drifts away.
He leaves behind him the ravished orange, which glints with pain.

Cathryn Elizabeth Reed (15)
St Mary's School, Cambridge

DEATH OF AN ORANGE

The sparkly, fiery, sphere revolving in my hand,
so innocent, so wondrous, a reflection in my eye.
The sharp hose, moves towards the light,
it stings the ball of fire and puts the bright flame out.
tears pour out, like some magical waterfall,
leaving it lifeless and severely dehydrated.
The flakes of ashes peel off the damaged structure,
revealing a fresh new zest, so sweet, yet so sour.
This new flame is not as sharp, or as beautiful,
but an old woman curled up in a rocking chair,
slowly dying, piece by piece,
as her insides break down, and crumble to bits.
This dying flame circle, splits into segments,
entering a new life, a new beginning.

Gökce Atamert (14)
St Mary's School, Cambridge

IT IS A SECRET!

Are there any peepers?
This story gives me the jeepers!
Should I tell you,
Rumours will start to grow too?
No, never mind,
There is someone listening in behind.
I cannot tell you, I will get in trouble,
Not even in a mumble.
Do not ask me to tell,
The person who it is about will shove me
                               down the well!

Sophie Davidson (13)
St Mary's School, Cambridge

HIS LONELY SHADOW

The lonely shadow,
Cast upon the hill,
Waits for the light,
To be banished away into sweet nothing.

As he follows the path,
Given to him by his leader,
He makes his way
Across the blank horizon.

The Earth's golden globe
Ascends slowly over the hill,
Diminishing this figure of darkness,
Into the world of non-existence.

Standing there, small, but invisible,
Still he waits,
Waits to be reincarnated,
Dressed in his robe of black.

Aya McLellan (14)
St Mary's School, Cambridge

A SLOWLY FADING MIST

He watched, paralysed,
as the key seized and grated in the lock,
around me a pale, still room, glazed with dullness.
In the corner stood a basin of blood,
trickling through the dark shadows.
A flickering gleam of obscurity grew,
from a long, sharp crack in the slowly fading mist.

Olivia Wallis (14)
St Mary's School, Cambridge

THE ROSEBUD

The sealed orange crust glints in the dazzling light,
Like an unopened rosebud with a secret land of layers,
The sharp steel is inserted as the tears overflow,
And the stranger of the knife starts to craft his work.

As the fresh zest sails through the stale air,
The delicate petals fall to the floor,
Revealing the centre covered in warm snow,
Slowly diminishing as the stranger rips away.

Vigorously the stranger tears the heart apart,
The enticing fruit slowly drifting away,
Never to be a complete rose again,
The bright, alluring shade now a distant memory.

Claire Davis (14)
St Mary's School, Cambridge

PREDATOR

He carefully examines the waxy face, slowly he inspects.
With a frown of concentration he takes the cold knife,
Sharply he jabs directly into the crown of his victim.
He makes his first incision, crafting with care.
He tears off the first of the leathery skin,
He's expressionless as he reveals the flesh.
Juices ooze through his tense fingers.
He devours a dripping sliver.
The fresh zest wafts in the stale air.
What a delicious orange!

Ella Siân McKee (14)
St Mary's School, Cambridge

ORANGE TEARS

He picks it up and inspects it,
He watches it hungrily.
Slowly he picks up the knife;
He watches it glint in the light,
Then carefully he plunges the knife into its body.
Tears flow out from within it.
They fall to the floor in a stream of pain.
He tears away its thick waxy skin
To reveal the soft segmented fruit.
He rips it apart.
Greedily he eats it, bit by bit,
The last of its tears dribbling slowly down his chin.
Finally all that is left of the orange is its skin,
He throws the skin to one side
And continues with his day.

Caroline Slack (14)
St Mary's School, Cambridge

MUSICAL SILENCE

I hear the gentle drone of the brightly-shining lights,
The chairs squeaking their own little tune,
The determined silence of thinking scholars,
A sudden cough like a blast from the throat,
The leaves rustling in the breeze,
Pens flowing gracefully over paper,
Great footsteps as if of a giant,
One violin playing to the world.

Corinna Guthrie (13)
St Mary's School, Cambridge

THE MURDER

As the stranger confirms his mission,
The waxy ball catches the light.
Contemplation dwells in the silence before
He stabs the thick oily skin vigorously
And rips it apart, segment by segment.
Expressionless the murder continues.
There are helpless calls receiving no reply.

The skin is peeled back with caution,
Revealing juicy segmented flesh,
The flimsy shell is discarded
And the juice runs through the man's fingers
Finally the predator indulges in his prey
By ripping a chunk out of the flesh.
Ending the hunger, the quest is terminated.

Rachel Steen (15)
St Mary's School, Cambridge

TAP-DANCING BUILDERS

Do you hear the tap-dancing builders banging metal drums?
Leaves whispering to one another as they sway in the wind?
The determined silence of thought drifting about the room?
One solitary violin playing out strongly to the world?
A thousand pens flowing effortlessly over stark white paper?
Birds chattering happily as they glide through the air?
Slow creaking chairs like old, old women?
The thunderous footsteps of a giant?

I do!

Bronwen Moore (13)
St Mary's School, Cambridge

THE WAXY ORANGE SPHERE

I sat and watched;
A man stood, inspecting his task.
The orange shone in the brightness of the light.
Then suddenly he stabbed it with a sharp glinting knife
And he started to craft the orange, and prise it open!

Then viciously, he pierced the orange again and again;
And it constantly gave out a rich juice of pain.
The skin was torn from its body
And the orange was sliced open, segment by segment.

Greedily he ate a large part of the fruit, in one gulp
And its helpless body was then thrown away!
Now nothing remains
But the smell of fresh zest that wafts in the stale air.

Tabitha Cassels (14)
St Mary's School, Cambridge

SILENCE

I hear the determined silence of life,
The sound of footsteps like a giant stomp across the road,
I hear the distant builders tap-dancing and others banging
on metal drums!
The next-door neighbour droning a flat tone to the world,
I hear the nearby wood swaying and trees whispering to each other,
The energetic woodpecker in the garden breaks the silence,
I hear the rumbling of the cars as they speed down the street,
The crying of children as they fall off the kerb,
I hear a sneeze from beside me like a gun on a shooting range
Dad
Again!

Susannah Hewett (13)
St Mary's School, Cambridge

WHAT I SAW

I saw a star trying to catch its tail.
I saw a man shining far away.
I saw a flower biting on his nails.
I saw a shadow in a beautiful colour.
I saw a pony playing on a wall.
I saw a stone enjoying the grass.
I saw a train lying on the beach.
I saw a chair speeding down the track.
I saw the sun falling to the ground.
I saw a platform heating up the town.
I saw a secretary painted in marble white.
I saw the ice cream talking on the phone.
I saw a cat melting in my hands.

Yaroslavna Simdyankina (13)
St Mary's School, Cambridge

THE PLANET ORANGE

The god of the planets inspects his quarry.
He prongs his piercing blade into the
North Pole of the Planet Orange.
As his piercing blade penetrates through the
South Pole, the Orange Sea splashes
its sweet sea in defence.
His spidery fingers peels the Orange Sea
and the cry of the Earth sets off a stream of lava.
There is greed in his eyes while he slowly
but vigorously dissects his victim.
In a gulp, Europe is gone and he gets ready
to take another continent.

Han Bin Lee (14)
St Mary's School, Cambridge

SILENCE

A large, draughty, unwelcoming room,
With rotting, whitewashed window frames,
The glass so dirty, it lets little light in.
A girl sits, desperately alone,
And nothing but the soft whispering of leaves
Penetrates the silence of the room,
A sound that she cannot hear.

The light is dimming,
Yet she sits, perseveres with the silence.
As the light continues to dwindle,
A thick black velvety darkness closes in on her,
She sits, unwanted, rejected from society.
Then her world changes,
Her silence is abruptly, disturbingly non-existent.

She can hear the sound of tap-dancing builders in the distance,
The faint murmur of a soulful violin,
Lights that drone a flat, tuneless melody,
A rocking chair that creaks, as if singing its own shrill tune,
Life is suddenly better,
She can hear.

Then the floor vibrates,
A persistent, loud, inexplicable banging,
Like giant footsteps,
The contentment of the dream trickles away,
Like water running down a gutter,
She hears no more.
Her world is devastatingly silent again.

Sarah Sheppard (13)
St Mary's School, Cambridge

SORRY

When I look around me,
All I see is you,
Your look, your touch, your eyes, your heart,
Your whole body's see-through

I look and look so hard,
I even strain my eyes,
But nothing hurts me more than,
Seeing all those lies.

You lie and lie and never stop,
You even lie to me,
But when it comes to telling you,
You never seem to see.

Can't you see I'm hurting,
You're hurting me so bad,
You couldn't even tell me,
But someone already had.

I really do love you,
And that is the truth,
But when it comes to you,
I really need some proof.

Why do you do this?
Why lie to me?
After all I've done for you,
I guess you just don't see.

Is it the way I treat you?
The way I wash your clothes?
The way I do the shopping?
No one really knows.

I don't know if I can forgive you,
For what you've done to me,
But I might be able to,
If you say that you're sorry.

Kerrin Bonwick (13)
St Peter's School, Huntingdon

ONE MOMENT IN STEPS

The atmosphere surrounded us,
we both said nothing.
All we did was stare at each other,
we spoke with our eyes,
not our mouths.

We stayed in that position from
nightfall till sunset.
I stayed impatient for my question
to be answered.

I thought to myself how much
longer could I wait?

Then I said to myself, 'What
must they be thinking?'
Both our eyes were sparkling
like a lump of gold,
They twinkled with each and every blink.

It was getting more and more
tense as time went by.
With every breath we took,
I could feel my heart getting warmer.

I felt like giving up,
when with a sigh of relief
In just that one second
I got my answer.
I couldn't believe what I saw.

It was a wink.
It had to be, I saw it with
my own two eyes.
I trusted my eyes enough to say
that it was a wink.

The wink wasn't any old wink.
It was a wink to bring out
the new start I had been
waiting for.

I have always dreamt
of this moment.
The day I became
independent.

It was the first time I had
ever felt this way.
It was true. It was real.
And I was . . .

Fatema Ahmed (13)
St Peter's School, Huntingdon

THE LAST TEMPTATION OF EVE

Behold the great Garden of Eden,
Where lived the ancestors of men and women.
Adam and Eve, the unique pair,
Whom God created with love and care.

They lived happily, a life with no woes.
With all our friends, with no foes.
If only they had that promise kept,
Now they'd always be in deep debt.

It all began with the spoilt angel, Lucifer,
He hungered after knowledge and power.
He betrayed God who then sent him to Hell,
Where he had to stay and forever dwell.

Of course he burst into a terrible rage,
He broke out from the fiery cage.
And he swore that he'd cause havoc on Earth,
Then there was the serpent, his new birth.

The serpent slithered on the grounds of Eden,
Where lived the ancestors of men and women,
And he saw the beautiful, stunning Eve,
Who was very easily deceived.

Gullible Eve saw him as a friend,
Recognising her innocence, he started to blend.
He then suggested 'Why don't we have some fruit?'
He pointed at one tree, Eve was mute.

At first, Eve explained that that fruit was forbidden,
But she couldn't bear the desire she had long hidden.
Adam was there too; he didn't say anything,
Despite the fact that he had the same longing.

One can't force another to give in,
Adam had the heart to defy. To win.
'It'll give you power and knowledge,' Lucifer hissed.
They bit it, all the light faded in the mist.

The wicked laugh of the serpent haunted Eden,
Where lived the ancestors of men and women.
But now it was only a land of all flaws.
Adam and Eve no longer heard God's calls.

Carmen Sett-Wong (14)
St Peter's School, Huntingdon

THE WOOD OF NIGHTMARES

There's a dark, dark wood inside my head,
Where the monsters of the night cry out in the moonlight,
Where zombies crawl out of the ground and devour all that pass them,
Where mad axe-men destroy trees to cut off your escape . . .

There's a dark, dark wood inside my head,
Where enormous dragons blow tornadoes of fire that destroy all in
    their path,
And where gruesome goblins with razor-sharp swords hack
    you to death on the leaf-soaked floor . . .

There's a dark, dark wood inside my head
Of demented headless horsemen trailing deadly creatures of the
    night behind their ghostly horses
And giant spiders hang you by your neck and werewolves eat
    your corpse with their daggered teeth,
        sinking deeper and deeper into every part of your body.

There's a dark, dark wood inside my head . . .

Nathan Holding (12)
Sawston Village College

A WINTER'S NIGHT

Spacious sky,
Dark and black.
Shimmering stars,
Glimmering moon.

Silence along the icy streets.
Warm glows from house to house.
Flickering brightness,
From small open doors.
Chilling wind howls,
Over frosty roads and paths.

Chills sweep along hedgerows and treetops.
Swaying them, side to side, as it swirls.
Ebony emptiness all around;
Frosted pathways, and snowfall.

Open to the warm and cosy home.
Fire lit, heat pouring out.
Nice warm bed,
Gazing up at the stars shining down.

Amy Greenstock (13)
Sawston Village College

A BLANK PAGE

The page is gonna get me,
I don't know what to do.
Ideas are flying at me,
And my head is filled with glue.

The teacher's coming over,
Look at what I've done.
My head remembers nothing,
But my poem's somehow begun.

I didn't write this poem,
It wasn't me, I swear.
'This is brilliant, fantastic,
Come up here and share.'

Richard Simpson (12)
Sawston Village College

NIGHTMARE

There's a dark, dark wood
inside my hollow head
where the night wind whistles
and the evils howl,
Werewolves, vampires, zombies too.
The stench of blood in the air,
the stench of blood on the earthy floor.

There's a dark, dark wood
inside my crazed head.
There's a bloodthirsty abductor
running wild and free.
The sudden single sound,
makes me leap
with a non-stop fear in my eyes.

There's a dark, dark wood
inside my head.
Hunting me all the way.
Oh, how I long
for a little glint of light,
but it's too late now . . .
I'm as dead as a doornail!

Lucy Deeming (12)
Sawston Village College

ONE DAY I'LL FLY AWAY

I had a dream, people liked me
I was popular, happy
Had no worries, no fears,
Then I awoke to reality
To face the day ahead
I try to think 'each day is new', 'anything could happen',
But it doesn't work, I know it's not true
Each day is the same
Each day is a nightmare
I walk to school, scared and with no one to talk to
I get to class and sit on my own
No friends, embarrassed, intimidated
People stare at me like I don't fit in
I want to change
What did I do to deserve this?
I spend the day on my own
Alone with my thoughts
Maybe it's all in my head
Maybe this is all a bad dream,
And I'll wake up happy as can be
I know this isn't true
I'm a victim
Soon it will end
The bullying won't,
But I will.

Emma Fuller (13)
Sawston Village College

BELIEVE YOUR DREAMS

A man once told me, believe your dreams
But there's no point because they never come true.
Of course they don't, where is fairyland
But in the dreams of me and you?

A man once told me, believe your dreams
Where wonders come from the tip top hill,
Where goblins shout here and there
Where pixies run around and thrill.

Lucy Goodchild (12)
Sawston Village College

THE TREASURES IN MY ROOM!

My room holds lots of treasure -
Not pirate treasure or jewels,
But treasure just as valuable.

The presents my friends gave me when I moved away:
My little furry kiwi, my pink and purple cushion;
My delicate china teddy sitting on a chair and my writing set.

There are things from far-off places,
Each as precious as gold.
My Mickey Mouse watch Dad bought for me when I went to Bali;
My little Korean girl wearing such pretty clothes;
My jar of gold I panned when I went to Sovereign Hill.

Then there are the treasures sitting on my shelf, all very special:
My Beatrix Potter moneybox and mug from when I was christened;
My collection of hippos, all different, but so cute;
My letterbox where I keep my writing stationery; my letters.
Safely tucked away I have my winning debating speech.

In my jewellery box are my first pair of earrings.
Somewhere there's my Christmas stocking,
Knitted with Granny's help.

My room holds lots of treasures.

Charlotte Duthie (12)
Sawston Village College

THE NIGHTMARE WOOD

There's a dark, dark wood
inside my head where the orcs prowl
heads hanging on trees and on wooden spikes.
My heart is pumping as the front headlights of a
BMW with a wooden spike attached to the front chaser, after me.
Giant spiders' webs with real people getting their heads
torn off by the spiders' claws.

There's a dark, dark wood
inside my head where the flesh-eating hands circle the trees.
Screams come from the centre of the forest.
I pass puddles of blood.
I hear branches snapping.

There's a dark, dark wood
inside my head where the zombies fall in giant wormholes
and walk into trees
Vampires guard the forest.
Goblins jump from tree to tree.

George Russell (12)
Sawston Village College

I'M NO GOOD

I'm not really very good at poetry,
My teacher comes out all clever and says a poem is,
'The best words in the best order,'
But I'm not really very good at poetry,
So when everyone settles down and writes their
                                limerick or tanka,
I sit there looking really blank thinking,
I'm not really very good at poetry.

Ashley Bennison (13)
Sawston Village College

NIGHT

Hypnotic,
dark, black,
night,
nightfall,
shade,
mine,
cavern,
sooty,
dungeon,
lightless,
starless,
indigo,
blue,
Prussian.
Overwhelming,
engulfing,
She's like a mother, gentle,
caring. With a thousand
children, stars glowing dark
in the night. Caressing, loving.

heat
lightened
day

warm
shadows
gloom

Alexandra Murphy (12)
Sawston Village College

THE MEETING

We are all gathered here to discuss . . .
What do you think of the matter . . .?
How do you feel about this . . .?
When should it go ahead . . .?
How shall we do it . . .?
Do we all agree . . .?
Snooze!

Liam Miller (14)
Sawston Village College

MY CAT

My cat has eyes as bright as fire
Whiskers that are long and quivering
And a purr as loud as a lawnmower.

My cat has sleek, warm, black fur
When he cuddles up on my lap.
My cat has shining, white teeth
To grasp its food and prey.

My cat has sensitive pointed ears
And a restless long tail.
My cat has a rough, bright pink tongue,
Which he delicately licks himself with.

My cat has long, scratching sharp claws
And soft padded paws.
My cat has a wet nose
To sniff his food.

My cat has a quiet miaow
That attracts your attention.
My cat has a flexible body
So he can jump high
And lick himself.

My cat is very beautiful
And all these things I have written.
I love *my cat!*

Olivia Tenberg (12)
Sawston Village College

FIRST DAY

A huge place,
Crowded with children,
Some my age, some not,
I cried on my first day.

No friends,
Towering buildings shadow me,
Nowhere to go,
I got lost on my first day.

Strange people look down at me
Pushing me around,
No one wants to be my friend,
I wanted to run away on my first day.

Huge rooms,
Open and crowded places,
Not able to find the dinner queue.
I went hungry on my first day.

Standing alone,
Benches are full,
Wandering aimlessly.
I was lonely on my first day.

Walking around,
Eating lunch,
Knowing everywhere to go.
I found friends on my second day.

Alistair White (13)
Sawston Village College

WAVE RIDER

Sleek, shiny, smooth, soft,
Gliding through the waves,
Riding the water like a horseman,
Wave Rider.

Bouncing, turning, jumping, diving,
Flying through the air,
Twisting high like a snowflake,
Wave Rider.

The dolphin explores the undersea life.
Shoals of multicoloured fish scuttle past,
Long, lanky strands of seaweed sweep the floor,
The floor that holds the treasure chest of
Shells and pearls and sand.

Streamlined, thin, long, graceful,
Time to end the glorious day.
Go to the seabed like a retired journeyman
Wave Rider.

Maya Bienz (12)
Sawston Village College

THE NIGHT

Excitement all around me
As the sun starts to set
It's time, I thought to myself
'It's time,' I said

My eyes grow wider
The shadows emerge
I'm excited, yet scared
But willing to go on

The stars and planets
Take over my soul
No more sunlight
Just sweet moonbeams

The moon is as bright as the sun
And in a way
More beautiful and mysterious
Guiding me through the night.

Claire Lampon (12)
Sawston Village College

THE NIGHTMARE WOOD

There's a dark, dark wood
Inside my head
Where nameless monsters rule the Earth
Where hungry vampires roam the sky
I try to escape these evil beings
But the road just gets longer and longer . . .

There's a dark, dark wood
Inside my head
With high-piercing shrieks from far beyond
I see a river of deep red blood flow past my feet
Now the piercing shrieks have stopped
I wonder why but then I realise . . .

There's a dark, dark wood
Inside my head
Where gruesome gallopers wander
The shrieking has started again
Another blood puddle passes by
I stop, turn around and run and I don't look back . . .

James Pugh (12)
Sawston Village College

THE NIGHT

Creeping through the silent streets
As the sun says its goodbye
Falling down under the horizon
And now the black is nigh

Darkness washing over light
Covering the silky sky
Out come the jewelled stars
While the sun will finally die

The moon stares at me knowingly
And I sit down on the path
His eyes watching me in the gloaming
The world captured in his wrath

I set off home in steady steps
Through the silent night
My shadow sweeping over the land
Like a bird in flight

I reach my house and slip inside
The silence cold and eerie
I fall into my bed, tuck up
Feeling tired, weary

Before I know it, dawn yawns
Pouring in the sunlight
The fear is gone, I'm safe for now
Till it comes again, the *night!*

Maryam Oghanna (12)
Sawston Village College

THE THIRTEENTH NATIVITY PLAY

Welcome one and all,
To a tale short and tall,
Upon a day in a shining way,
Of the thirteenth nativity play.

The fairy's on the donkey,
The presents laugh with glee,
The Gabriel's star's gone wonky,
And everyone looks at me.

I'm the only one that looks right,
The others all look wrong,
And *bang!* I was hit on the head,
By a Jesus with no clothes on.

That's Mary, Joe and the Wise Men down,
The others soon to follow,
Oops, that he hit was Herod's crown,
Then a cry, a yelp and a bellow.

It's hot in all this cotton wool,
It's my turn now, 'Baa, baa.'
My family start to clap and cheer,
To them I am the star!

Farewell one and all,
From a tale short and tall,
Upon a day in a shining way,
Of the thirteenth nativity play.

Charley Collier (12)
Sawston Village College

MY GRANDMOTHER

My grandmother sits in her armchair and stares
At the world through the eyes of a terrified child;
Everywhere alien sensations surround her,
Silent confusion behind her wide eyes so empty,
It hurts my heart to see her so lonely, yet,
Surround by the friends and family she does not know.
A shell of the lady who gave birth to my mother, she knew me once,
She could know me again but that will never be.
What has she done to deserve such a cruel fate worse than death?
Mother, lover, charity worker, carer, please don't go.
I know that you are dying but I know that you'll never be gone,
Because the lady who cradled me in her arms as a baby,
With her pink leather handbag and little pink purse,
She will never be gone from our hearts and our minds,
More than just one more cherished victim of Alzheimer's deadly curse.

Jonathan Whale (15)
Sawston Village College

STORM

Lightning strikes, thunder storms
All the while rain clashes to the ground.
The mud splatters and the sky crackles,
Like an old witch brewing a storm.
The wind is whistling and the trees are rustling,
All the while rain clashes to the ground.
Light flashes now and then,
With a distant scream from the sky.
The cold seeps through the walls,
Choking you with the wind on its side.
All the while the rain clashes to the ground.

Laura O'Keeffe (13)
Sawston Village College

THE JET-BLACK NIGHT

The violent wind howls, blowing everything into a whirling despair,
the dark transforms every object around it to a sinister silhouette.

Wispy trees linger around like gangly, cryptic fingers,
tapping at my bedroom window longing to come in.

The moon illuminates the darkness around us enclosing
everything, making it become an eerie, icy atmosphere.

Every narrow alleyway is patrolled by dangerous predators
that linger, for any innocent, vulnerable victim.
Their breath oozes out like clouds of poison in the gloomy air.

Am I safe?

I think I know that I'm safe. It is the dangerous jet-black night
and I'm tucked up warm and tight.

Rebecca Fordham (12)
Sawston Village College

THE KILLER

Swiftly he comes
his eyes sharp and staring
almost invisible in the dark night.
Then, he sees her and slows to a walk.
He creeps up behind her and grabs her throat
forcing her into an empty street.
A flash of silver, she falls to the ground.
With a bolt like lightning he disappears.
She wakes up with doctors over her
and knows instantly what has happened.
The cancer inside her has attacked her heart again.
Fear, the death is near.

Natasha Edwards (13)
Sawston Village College

OFF THE BUS

Off the bus and to our forms
With our shirts tucked in and our collars out
We wander from building to building
Meeting our friends and stopping to chat -
Then running when the bell goes
Science next - or maybe maths
Better check or we'll be late!

Break time now - what shall we do?
Sit on the bench or go to the shop?
Was that the bell?
Quick - run!
It's music next, then art
Maroon blurs flash by
As I run past.

Then suddenly - where am I?
Around me a few people are wandering astray
I'm lost! I'm lost!
Then, I hear someone shouting -
Calling my name.
I turn and see my brother
And the next thing I know
My brother is leading me to my next lesson.

Lunch! Great!
Mouth-watering smells waft through the air
Making my stomach rumble and my mouth run dry
I sit down and eat - food - yum!
Only two more long lessons!

At last - home time!
Everyone lining up - waiting for the bus
Then, around the corner the bus appears
And we wave goodbye
But we'll be back tomorrow!

Katie Wright (11)
Sawston Village College

THE BIN

In the bin I love to dig,
in amongst the flies,
to pick up fags and plastic bags,
until I find my prize.

First I search for squishy stuff,
as it's far, far greater,
and then I go down to the floor,
to find old mashed potato.

I can't really explain it but,
the good stuff gets down to the middle,
and flies like apples more than pears,
and many another riddle.

  I always find my homework,
when the day is nearly gone,
just to throw away again,
as the cycle moves on.

When I've finally given up,
I really look a fright,
I get cleaned up and go to sleep,
until another night.

Gregory Pugh (11)
Sawston Village College

THE NIGHTMARE

There's a dark, dark wood
Inside my head
Where the gloaming night noises rustle
Where the deadly, dangerous men whistle
And the vampire bats lurk around in the sky
Where children scream
Deafening and soundless.

There's a dark, dark wood
Inside my head
Where there's a bloodthirsty zombie
Waiting to commit slaughter.
Wounded people cry in the distance
As they smell the hunger of the beast.

There's a dark, dark wood
Inside my head
A slaying horseman canters by
Searching through the heart of the forest
For his victim
But finds no meat and retreats hungrily
To his devilish den.

Liam Flynn (12)
Sawston Village College

THE SNOW PONY

It's lonely in the winter,
I'm locked out by myself,
No warm rugs for comfort,
No human to welcome,
No comfy straw to lie on,
To rest my aching feet.

It's lonely in the winter,
All my food has gone,
The snow has claimed everything,
My stable, my shelter,
My protection, my life,
The snow has covered me.

It was lonely in the winter.

Jo Webster (13)
Sawston Village College

DARK, DARK WOOD

There's a dark, dark wood
Inside my head
Where the howling wolf cries
Where the trees all look the same
And where zombies follow you
Wherever you go
And screams echo around.

There's a dark, dark wood
Inside my head
Where the mossy tree roots catch your feet
And the spider never stops weaving to catch misled prey
In the centre there is a lake
Full of fears and frightening things.

There is a dark, dark wood
Inside my head
Where ghostly green goblins prowl
Sneakily, slyly from tree to tree
Where the hooting eagle owl calls out
Into the silent, eerie night
Where the haunted headless horseman gallops all year round.

Jennifer Mary Danes (12)
Sawston Village College

MY FIRST SIX WEEKS

On the way to school
my heart is racing
like a whirlwind spinning round

And everyone knows
where to go
all apart from me

The bell screams
bleep, bleep
lots of pushing and shoving

And all around
robots are busy
all wearing the same thing

I'm by myself
empty playground
buildings tower over me

The buildings laugh
Ha, ha, you're lost
You can't find your room

But my friends are marching
Like a colony of ants
The right room, that's where they're going

Time for lunch
my tummy's rumbling
the lunch queue a mile long

Last lesson
seems like hours
lots of endless writing

And there's my mum
smiling and happy,
'Hi Mum, it's been a great day.'

Bethany Pearce (11)
Sawston Village College

THE HUNT

The hunter stood
And mounted his horse
And if he could
He'd pass this hunting course

The fox was scared
While running wild
She only cared
About her unborn child

The hunter had seen it
In the light of the dawn
He had his torch lit
And blew his hunting horn

The fox turned and ran
Faster this time
The hounds caught up
End of the line!

The fox was in pain
Being ripped in half
It isn't a game
It's a vicious bloodbath!

Sam Grant (13)
Sawston Village College

THE WOOD OF NIGHTMARES

There's a dark, dark wood
inside my head where the mutant creatures
play with my helpless fears.
Where I hear endless moans and groans echo
from nowhere and where decapitated arms
reach up through the earth and drag you under.

There's a dark, dark wood inside my head
where vampire bats screech,
thirsty for human blood.
Where tree branches tap you on the back,
and where ghostly shadows seem to arise
from beneath the thick heavy fog.

There's a dark, dark wood inside
my head where demons linger round every corner
where spirits' whispers are carried through
the air on drifts of mist.
Where I am lost in my own nightmares.

Rosie Ball (12)
Sawston Village College

MY WORST NIGHTMARE

There's a dark, dark wood inside my head,
where I hear long-lasting screams of agony,
and the sweet taste of blood in the air,
where the horrific headless horsemen roam the planet,
where gruesome goblins lurk in trees.

There's a dark, dark wood inside my head,
where vile vampires come out to play,
and decapitated heads fall to the ground,
where werewolves howl their deadly song.

There's a dark, dark wood inside my head,
where ghastly zombies follow me,
and crazed axemen creep up on me,
where dangerous escaped prisoners capture me
from behind!

Jessie Loveday (12)
Sawston Village College

NIGHT FOREST

There's a dark, dark wood inside my head
Where the owls cry and tortured people howl in pain
Where the air is full of blood scents and dust
In a place where all the zombies horde their food
Where all the spirits rest in peace.

There's a dark, dark wood inside my head
Where soulless beasts lurk in the wood
Where werewolves howl on the moonlit hill
Where bodies are hanging hours on end
And a place where orcs protect their shacks.

There's a dark, dark wood inside my head
Where buzzards eat the dead meat
In a cemetery where bones with flesh still on them
Stick out of the ground
Where imps laugh at the stranded dead bodies
Where headless horsemen hunt down the beasts.

There's a dark, dark wood inside my head
Where the werewolves' claws strike at my heart
Where the buzzards watch and wait
Where the beasts are ready to feast
Until slowly my eyes start to close.

Marcus Wiley (12)
Sawston Village College

MY AFRICAN BOX

(Based on 'Magic Box' by Kit Wright)

In my African box I will put . . .
The seven shades of the rainbow,
A splash from Victoria Falls,
And three rays of the mighty tropical sun.

In my African box I will put . . .
The roar from a lion,
The beat of African music playing gently in my ear,
And the singing of the crickets at dusk.

In my African box I will put . . .
All the delicate petals from the blossoms,
The biggest pothole ever,
And the sound of dogs barking at night.

My African box will be created from . . .
A unicorn horn,
An African fish eagle's tail feather,
Some sparkles of gold,
Some crystals,
And a touch of magic.

Sophie Graham (12)
Sawston Village College

NIGHT

Night is like a comforting black sheet,
Where everything inside of it
Is peaceful and tranquil and there is no pressure
And no worries.

Night is like a ginormous bathtub of relaxation,
Where everything is comforting,
Calm, relaxing, cleansing and deeply soothing.

Night is like a room without any doors,
Where troubles and worries
Are shut out leaving happy thoughts and
Good feelings.

Night is like the Titanic not sinking,
Saving us from
The troubles of the day and shoving them to the side,
Delivering us to safety.

Sam King (12)
Sawston Village College

THE COMPUTER'S LOVE POEM

I am the love computer,
I have my own language,
I will connect to you in a special way!
Save me
Look at me
Repeat
But don't undo me.
Print me on your heart,
Attach me to you.
Copy my screen,
Merge me
Into your memory.
Detect and repair
The damage,
Help me
With your love.
Make me bold
And spellcheck me
Whatever you do
Read me right.

Daisy Ives (12)
Sawston Village College

SNOW

It flutters down,
drifts down,
pours down,
floats down.

White and crusty,
soft and powdery,
icy,
cold,
but fun to play in.

Beautiful, dangerous,
Frightening, soothing.

Make an igloo,
a snowman, a snowball,
from the white that
flutters down,
drifts down,
pours down,
floats down.
Snow.

Lesley McDermid (13)
Sawston Village College

FOOD

I love to eat food
I like food in my belly
Got a cupboard full of food
With a bowl full of jelly
Like butter on my toast
Ketchup on my chips

Gravy on my roast
And those little messy dips
I love to eat food
I like food in my belly
Got a cupboard full of food
With a bowl full of jelly.

Gemma Holmes & Samantha (12)
Sawston Village College

THE BLACK CAT

I watched from my window
And saw
A black cat
Slinking through the night like a panther.

As I watched from my window,
The black cat
Drew the darkness on
Like a leader going into battle.

From my window I saw
The blackest shadow
Creep onwards
Winning the battle and suffocating the day.

The black cat saw from his place on the ground
The moon,
Flag of his victory,
Darkness over day.

Joanna Byers (13)
Sawston Village College

NIGHT POEM

Sometimes I lie awake
Listening to the sounds of the night.
You can hear the distant sounds of clubs,
The car horns beeping loudly.

It's funny really,
Sometimes you could almost think
That night is busier than day
But then again I can't imagine that's true.

I don't like the night,
It makes me shiver coldly
My bed and quilt turn to stone
And someone whispers in my ear:

'You stupid child
What's your point?
Night is when all things good come out to play
And ghostly people haunt

Night is vivid,
Wild and free
Like a black bat
Hunting for juicy blood

And do you know what?
Sometimes the black bat
Will come up to your window,
Fly straight through and suck your blood

Believe me,
Not a pleasant sight
So don't be scared my child
Otherwise you won't be here tomorrow.'

Sophie Wiesner (12)
Sawston Village College

DARK, DARK WOOD

There's a dark, dark wood
inside my head
where white wolves howl
and skull-dragging escapees
pull their balls and chains behind them
where dark screams are often
and a while later
the taste of sour blood.

There's a dark, dark wood
inside my head
where a headless, howling horseman
prowls to find its deadly meal
where rats creep skilfully
around and in my mud-ridden feet
where small snakes creep
sneakily around.

There's a dark, dark wood
inside my head
where the smell is so hard
it breaks big branches off trees
where mud is sloppy
and grass all rocky
where bears lurk gruesome
and deadly around
that's what's inside my head.

Simon Chapman (12)
Sawston Village College

THE COMPUTER LOVE POEM

Turn on my power!
Be my office assistant!
Be my shadow!
Browse me!
Check me!
Choose my style!
Come into my window!
Comment on me!
Control me!
Customise me!
Edit me!
Enter your floppy into my drive!
Log me on!
Make me an attachment!
Make me fill your screen!
Make me your heading!
Merge with me!
Nudge me!
Press my buttons!
Press my number lock button!
Put me on your desk!
Restore me!
Save me in your file!

Richard Simpson & Daniel Badcock (12)
Sawston Village College

ONE DAY . . .

One day I think I'll change the world.
Make everything more me.
I'll turn the sky a shade of pink
And let the pigs fly free.

One day I think I'll change the world.
Make everything more me.
One day I'm going to change the world
Just you wait and see.

Jessica Smith-Lamkin (12)
Sawston Village College

NIGHT

Night is just the absence of colour,
Not pitch-black and blindness.
A welcome cloak over the eyes,
Protecting them from unwanted light.

Night is opposite to day,
Still and calm, quiet and peaceful.
A time to rest your eyes
And think of the day you've endured.

Night's for reflecting and musing,
To imagine, ponder and brood.
A time to plan for the future
And use your mind and not your hands.

Night's a friend who won't breathe a word,
To whom you can empty your mind
And leave it free from all pressures,
Never telling a single soul.

Night is just the absence of colour,
Not pitch-black and blindness.
A welcome cloak over the eyes,
Protecting them from unwanted light.

Ruth Pritchard (12)
Sawston Village College

NIGHTMARES IN A FOREST!

There's a dark, dark wood inside my head
Where the wounded cry
Where the nameless monsters lurk
Where orcs and axemen meet escaped prisoners
And the sour stench of blood is in the air.

There's a dark, dark wood inside my head
Spiders creep and crawl around in the undergrowth
Leeches suck the blood of the dead
Tarantulas patrol this forest of nightmares
Now there's no escape . . .!

There's a dark, dark wood inside my head
Where blood and bones and guts are strewn
Where the screams of the deformed wake the dead
As the screeching sound of tearing skin
Leaps around in the wood,
Or is this all just in my head?

Jennifer Tweed (12)
Sawston Village College

CHEWING GUM

Chewing gum is banned from school
Don't know why, it's a very strict rule
Chewing gum's great -
Some people's best mate
Tastes good
Like it should
Makes teeth nice and white
Sparkly and immensely bright
Makes your breath all nice and minty
Lasts a long time and there is plenty.

Bai-ou He (13)
Sawston Village College

NIGHTMARE

There's a dark, dark wood inside my head
Where the ghastly green goblins prowl
And the screaming headless horseman gallops
Trailing unspeakable terrors behind him.

There's a dark, dark wood inside my head
Where my ferocious fears are scattered everywhere
The dense, drab forest possessed by my demons.

There's a dark, dark wood inside my head
Where the willow weeps and the rook nests
And my nightmares are put to rest.

James Doherty (12)
Sawston Village College

DAYDREAMING

She stands, waits,
Staring into the mists,
A bus comes and goes,
She's away in her own land,
A land of peace and quiet,
Away from the hustle and bustle of the town,
From the barging people, the screaming children,
The cars, the bikes, the trains,
A land of peace and quiet,
Another bus comes and goes,
Staring into the mists,
She stands,
Waits.

Kerry Chapman (14)
Sawston Village College

SPILL MY SECRET

You're so annoying,
You special little whisper,
I can't tell of you,
'Cause you won't be a secret anymore if I did,
So unwelcome you are in my mind,
I really don't know what to do with you,
What are you up to?
I know you too well.
You're bursting, I know it
'Cause I am too,
This is your fault not mine,
. . . Right that's it!
I can't help myself, I have to spill,
Oh, how well I tried to keep you,
All to myself
But I can't,
You're just too special to keep.

Helen Akther (13)
Sawston Village College

HERE SHE COMES

Here she comes,
Dressed in black,
Creeping silently,
Like a cat.

Here she comes,
With her dim lantern,
Shining down,
High in the sky.

Here she comes,
'Quick,'
Someone said,
'Run, hide!'
Once again,
The sun has died.

Dan Hunter (13)
Sawston Village College

NIGHTMARE WOOD

There's a dark, dark wood
Inside my head,
Where decapitated heads hang
Gruesomely from trees
On a piece of blood-ridden rope
And green gremlins lurk hungrily
In the tree roots.
I can see enormous tarantulas
Ready to feast.
I see trails of blood
And hear piercing screams in the distance.
Where in the eerie shadowiness of the wood
Strange and unknown creatures hide.

There's a dark, dark wood
Inside my head,
Where a crazed, headless horseman
Gallops frantically past me,
Where vampires prowl for wounded victims,
Where a devilish sky haunts me!

There's a dark, dark wood
Inside my head . . .

Viki Fuller (12)
Sawston Village College

No One Lives Forever

It comes upon you.
You can't see it but it's there.
Walking among us.
Then it strikes.
All hell breaks loose.
Then it stops, no beating the cold silence.
It has claimed another victim.
It comes in the cold, when you least expect it.
Families are upset, crying, asking why them, why now?
It's not a man-made thing, it's natural.
Everyone will be struck down in the end.
No one can stop it.
No one is immortal.
Because death takes you away.
You never know when you're going to go.
No one lives forever.

Sophie Pettit (14)
Sawston Village College

The Flash

Its subtle wings slice the unfortunate air,
The tip is varnished by its own heat,
The flames of the creature's back
Roars as it prowls near its target.
It stops.
The target sleeps for five more seconds.
It drops.
It's too late for all people
The flash . . .
      The mushroom . . .
        The death.

Tim Baker (13)
Sawston Village College

NIGHTMARE WOOD

There's a dark, dark wood
inside my head,
where the night orcs hunt,
where the werewolves howl,
and the gremlins hide.
Where zombies roam
and trails of fresh, dark blood
lead to nowhere.

There's a dark, dark wood
inside my head,
where horrifying, headless horsemen gallop,
leading deadly goblins behind them.
Where nameless monsters
mask their gruesome faces
and where beastly nightmares
lurk by winding tree roots.

There's a dark, dark wood
inside my head,
where the wind rustles the trees
and ghostly shadows emerge.
Where the spiders' beaded webs
raise the hairs on a wanderer's neck
and where phantasmal creatures
wander the ferny ground.

Sam Jeffrey (12)
Sawston Village College

FIRST DAY

'Get out the door *now* - look at the time!'
Made it to the bus stop just in time.
Show him the bus pass, jump aboard,
Bumping along the muddy road.

Raining, pouring, wet rain, heavy rain,
Splashing all around.
Mucky, noisy, scary, worry,
Mud all over the ground.

Big books, heavy books, old books, new books,
Teachers, strict and kind.
Tall kids, short kids, noisy kids, quiet kids,
Wallets, lose and find.

Break time - phew.

Kids all charging around,
Fallen onto the ground.
Maybe I could use a vender -
Can I find a money-lender?

Maths and history, science and geography,
Art and drama, PSE.
English and RE, languages and PE,
Music, IT and DT.

Pizza, nuggets, what should I take?
Great big choccytoffy cake!
Looks like Titanic in a sea of custard -
Think I'll have a burger - extra mustard.

Great big buildings reaching up like trees,
Fallen over and hurt my knee.
'Collars! Collars!' teachers yell,
Three-two-one, it's time for the bell!

Chaaaarge!
Phew!
Uh-oh!
Homework.

Mark Jackson (11)
Sawston Village College

A DARK, DARK WOOD

There's a dark, dark wood inside my head
where werewolves howl, where vampires prowl
leaving trails of their victims' blood.
Where gremlins hide amongst tree roots
waiting to pounce on anything that passes them
and ear-piercing screams never end.

There's a dark, dark wood inside my head
where every tree is alive
where zombies' hands grab my feet
where tarantulas cover the floor like a carpet
where strange sounds are carried in from north, east, south and west
and never seem to stop.

There's a dark, dark wood inside my head
where decapitated heads hang from branches
where mad axemen roam round waiting to kill
and headless horsemen scare all night long.
If you go in you never come out
but suffer in fear and eternal torment.

Dean Miller (12)
Sawston Village College

FIRST DAY OF COLLEGE

On the bus it's never quiet,
Always riots going on.
Then there's us sitting quietly,
Only riots on the bottom,
Then there's up at the top.

We have our passes to get on
At the bus stop in the morning,
I'm the only Year 7 girl.
No one to talk to till on the bus,
Pretty boring if you ask me.

Then we get to school.
It's all so daunting.
I forget where my form room is,
I'm worried about getting lost,
There are so many different teachers,
Different buildings and different pupils.
Some tall Year 11s make fun of you
And spit on the ground!

But the overall verdict is - cool school!

Gemma Hollidge (11)
Sawston Village College

FIRE

Leaping flames from a tiled roof
The smoke billowing up high
Water spraying from a hose
Smells fill the air.

Windows break, glass everywhere
You can feel the rising heat
Fire engines make a noise
Bang as something explodes.

Black and dirty firemen work
Trying to save what's left
Hopelessly digging through
Oh, what a mess.

Victoria Wallace (14)
Sawston Village College

A DREAMER'S NIGHTMARE

There's a dark, dark wood
Inside my head
Where unknown creatures lurk
and there are deadly, threatening whispers
Shadows of crazed horsemen gallop
Zombies, like phantoms stalk

There's a dark, dark wood
Inside my head
Where there're haunted, endless gateways
leading to a screaming graveyard.
Allotments owned only by a mad axeman
Never seen, never heard.

There's a dark, dark wood
Inside my head
Where ghostly, green goblins snigger
as their prey draws nearer.
Trees move closer to me
Their branches leaning over spitefully
To grab me.

There's a dark, dark wood
Inside my head . . .
a very dark, dark wood.

Emma Cracknell (12)
Sawston Village College

ESCAFLOWNE

She said she came from Earth,
They said she came from the Mystic Moon,
She came from the Pillar of Light,
But nobody knew why

It was the fate alteration machine,
That the Zaibuch Empire made,
Evil Lord Daunkirk wanted the Ideal Future
But the dragon still overshadowed it,
Nobody knew why

Allen loved Hitomi, and she him,
Vulcan loved Aeria, and she him,
But Van loved Hitomi, and Naria loved Vulcan,
Daunkirk had changed fate,
But Van and the dragon would stop him,
The dragon, Escaflowne, and Hitomi were special,
But nobody knew why

Asturia stopped Zaibuch,
And Vulcan slayed Daunkirk
Allen fell in love with Milerna
Hitomi loved Van now,
Vulcan, Nara and Aeria were dead
But Hitomi still went back to the Mystic Moon
And nobody knew why.

Judith Kendall (13)
Sawston Village College

MRS DALLAWAY

Down the dark and dusty road,
Through the old and rusty ivy,
Lives Mrs Dallaway.

She lives alone,
A widow for so long,
Lives Mrs Dallaway.

After school I tread,
Along the haunted road,
To Mrs Dallaway's.

Her place smells of cats,
Her garden of old socks,
Lives Mrs Dallaway.

Her cooking is so old-fashioned,
Her furniture the same,
But that's Mrs Dallaway.

I dream and wait,
For the hour I'm let out,
From Mrs Dallaway's.

The journey home feels wonderful,
Back to my heavenly home,
Goodbye Mrs Dallaway.

Jessie Radcliffe-Brown (11)
Sawston Village College

SOLDIER'S GRAVE

Too many men are wasted,
too many names are pasted
upon the cemetery stones.
And what gain
is worth this pain
upon one man's brittle bones?

Too much hurt cannot be cured,
too much to be endured
by the families of the dead,
for those survivors of the terrible scenes
cannot comprehend quite what it means,
as they take breath in the sea of red.

The easiest way to end it
would be to not contend it
and to proudly admit defeat.
Never practised is this idea
because of man's fear
his name will be on the concrete.

Robin Byatt (13)
Sawston Village College

NIGHT

The darkness swoops down like a bird,
its beady eye, a diamond in the midnight sky.
Its wings suffocate the outside world,
its heart beats like footsteps in the dark.

The darkness leaks in from the ceiling,
like a tap, dripping deadly water.
It slowly fills the room with an eerie silence,
I drown in a midnight blanket.

The darkness prowls through the window like a tiger,
shredding the light with its gleaming claws.
It smothers me with its towering shadow
and cuts the deathly quiet with its tail.

Eleanor Moore (12)
Sawston Village College

NIGHT

I tread down the lonely path
Stepping on moonlit bracken
Pearl-covered spiders' webs
Inky-black heavens
Dotted with cotton wool clouds
And peeping gold stars
That twinkle and twinkle
Reflected from far.
Twigs break underfoot
And the grasshoppers click
A toad or frog croaking,
Click, croak, click.
A dirty stream running by
While pebbles jump and leap along
And a crashing waterfall, down there
With a distant church gong.
A rat burrowing in the ground
And a fox slinking behind a tree
A gentle badger nosing around
And an owl hooting at me.
Molten gold leaking from clouds
Stars cowering behind the day
Blackness sucked into the sky
As the dawn breaks, the day is laid.

Victoria Paulding (12)
Sawston Village College

CAT'S EYES

A black cat slunk across the path
Turning daylight into a silver glow,
Beams of star-studded light
Flicked across her back.

She turned her head
And her piercing gaze
Tore the twilight,
And restored the darkness.

And her eyes, her eyes,
The night's cold curiosity
Its fury and its peace,
Were reflected in her eyes.

And with one flick
Of her sleek, elegant tail
The moon awakened,
She turned her proud head towards it
And mewed with satisfaction.

Then all was quiet,
The sun rose to greet the morning,
Daylight took its hold
And the cat slunk away.

Clara Woolford (12)
Sawston Village College

THE BLACK CAT

The black cat was there.
He creeps around,
The stars are the mice he hunts at night.
The black cat crawls like a puma.

He was there.
The black cat was a sneaky cat,
He was a very furious, fast cat.
The black cat was the night!

Samantha Collings (12)
Sawston Village College

THE TEACHER

Shouting out for silence
Slams the ruler on the desk
Bratty children everywhere
Head spinning for a rest.

Run to the staffroom
Pick up the tea
Run to the next lesson
Oops, forget the key!

Running out of patience
Starting to lose her mind
Taking it out on all the kids
She used to be so kind!

Loads of extra homework
Tracking points galore
Lessons sat in silence
Merits don't exist anymore.

The class drives her crazy
She suddenly walked out
They all throw a party
It's brilliant without a doubt!

Laura Foster (13)
Sawston Village College

In My Room

In my room there's clothes.
In my room there's shoes.

In my room there's letters.
In my room there's footballs.

In my room there's ghosts.
In my room there's rubbish.

In my room there's money.
In my room there's hair gel.

In my room there's combs.
In my room there's toys.

In my room there's a bed.
In my room there's cupboards.

In my room there's a TV.
In my room there's a PlayStation.

Shaun Poulter (11)
Sawston Village College

Monster?

It comes out at night
And creeps around the house,
I've never really seen it,
But I'm sure it's there.
It leaves dusty footprints,
Leading to the door.
Is it blue? Green? Hairy? Dirty?
Big? Small? Alive? Dead?
I don't know, but it's under my *bed!*

Tom Perkins (11)
Sawston Village College

WHY?

Why is a fat man fat?
Why is a bat called that?
Why does the other queue move faster?
Why is the world so full of disaster?
Why does it rain when I wanna go out?
Why do teachers always shout?
Why when I'm happy are others glum?
Why do adults never have fun?
Why is it always, 'wait 'til you're older,'?
Why when it's hot does it always get colder?
Why does chocolate always melt?
Why do jeans only fit with a belt?
Why am I never right?

Alex Cracknell, Becki Grant & Rachel Pilsworth (12)
Sawston Village College

WHAT'S THAT OVER THERE?

Green, wet, shimmering, grass, shiny,
shining as the sun comes out,
I wonder if anyone's about.
Whatever it is, it's over there,
I can see its long ginger hair.
It's pouncing, jumping up the mound,
Its bell's making a twinkling sound.
It's seen something in the grass,
It's not happy, should I ask?
It's coming nearer to its prey,
Everyone look away.
I think that's enough for one day.

Zoey Demartino (11)
Sawston Village College

THE CELEBRITY

The celebrity steps out of the Audi TT,
He's walking on the red carpet, I wish it was me.

Another one comes out of a limousine,
I wonder where they're going, or where they've been?

People with cameras frantically clicking,
Not signing autographs as time is ticking.

They enter the building and take a seat,
They get a luxurious meal to eat.

One wins an award, he steps up on stage,
Other contestants stare with rage.

He walks away with his golden prize,
He's so happy, he almost cries.

He leaves the building and gets into the TT,
He goes back to his penthouse. I wish it was me!

Michael Ford (13)
Sawston Village College

THE FIGURE

I stood in the moonlight
Alone
I heard footsteps
It was all I could hear
I looked behind me
There was a figure
Who it was I did not know

I ran
Ran till it hurt
All I could hear was
Thump, thump, thump of my heart
I looked back
The figure had gone
I stood in the moonlight
Alone.

Alice Tasker (11)
Sawston Village College

NIGHT

Great clouds roam the sky like shadowy ghosts
Attacking wizened oaks with colossal lightning bolts
Creaking trees resemble thunderclaps
seeking to crash and ring with fear
As the Devil in his chariot of fire tears across the broken night sky

The darkness enveloped me, swallowed me
Bringing me ever closer to the unnerving cavern of a moonless sky
The stars, the only consoling lights in the sky
Were being pushed back by huge, black arms
that never seemed to cease in their everlasting quest

The endless wind seemed to wake the night into another round
of this never-ending fight
Enclosed in a deafening ring of sound
That spurred the night on like an angry crowd.

Matthew Drury (12)
Sawston Village College

THEN AND NOW

As I wander across the land,
I look out at the sea and sand,
The hills around me quiet as a mouse,
The sign of no one, no village, no house.
It's hard to imagine that years before
This countryside was the centre of war
And gunshots fired, right over your head
And you fell down dying, dead.
When I see only rabbits and deer
I can't imagine the screaming and fear,
Soldiers marching, faces alert,
Defending their country, hiding their hurt.
Two different countries, both aiming to kill,
Both sides scattered over this hill,
Not thinking of the damage that they'll create,
Not knowing of the devastation - until it's too late.
But now I know, their feelings are shared,
From that life-changing day war was declared,
So 20 years later when I stand here brave,
I think of the soldiers that fell to their graves.

Natasha Demartino (13)
Sawston Village College

MY ALIEN PARENTS

My parents are like aliens
Especially my dad.
He gets his yellow false teeth out
It makes me really mad.

My mum is just so crazy
She drives me up the wall.
It makes me really, really mad
Cos I'm not really that small.

My parents are like aliens
Believe me or not
And my mum is always on the phone
Speaking so non-stop!

Jessica Donald (11)
Sawston Village College

THE BLUE WOLF

The moon is ghostly against the ink-black sky,
The wolf looks blue in the pale light.
A tear runs down his blood-covered face,
As he howls his final goodbye.

His pack, his family, howl in reply,
And sadly whimper a whine.
The new pack leader rises up
And eyes the pack he owns.

The scar around his silver eye,
Glints in the light of the stars.
His once white fur is now blood-red
And matted down, not smooth.

He barks to his pack, 'Rejoice, rejoice,
For I am now in charge.'
Reluctantly they cry, 'Rejoice,'
And howl to the moon and stars.

When the light of the bright orange sun,
Is glimpsed from behind the rock,
The wolves creep back into their dens
And kiss their cubs goodnight.

Gracinda Colaço (12)
Sawston Village College

THE ATTACK

I was lying in bed when the ground started shaking,
The earth was vibrating, people started waking,
People were screaming, shouting for their children,
Some were shouting, 'Saddam's going to kill you!'

I was too scared to move as I heard crashes outside,
I covered my eyes to block out the noise,
I felt a hand grab me and pull me out of bed,
'Quick,' someone screamed, 'or else you'll be dead.'

I was rushed outside to be greeted by my family,
The shaking had stopped but the surroundings were wrecked badly,
Everyone was emotional, weeping and crying,
Some were saying, 'People must be dying.'

There was smoke in the air and flames in the distance,
One man said Hussein couldn't hold out the resistance,
He had bombed my city and killed hundreds of people,
Is it too much to ask just to be peaceful?

Lucy Squire (14)
Sawston Village College

BEASTS

Lions and tigers hunting the beast,
Getting ready for their next feast.

Leaping antelope ran from capture,
Meat and eat, caught by nature.

Zebra flee across the proud lands,
But hunters feed upon their glands.

Alice Whale (12)
Sawston Village College

Seasons

Spring is a time of the new year.
A time of school beginning.
The time of sky-blue skies.

Summer is the arrival of Hell's heat.
Summer is a time of laughter.
Summer is a time of happy holidays.

Autumn is a time of school opening again.
Autumn is a time of children collecting conkers.
Autumn is a time of people shivering.

Winter is a time of building snowmen.
Winter is a time of skidding on ice.
Winter is a time of opening Christmas stockings.

Muhmin Ahmed (12)
Sawston Village College

The Twin Towers

The Twin Towers collapsed
With 5000 people inside.
They ran and ran and ran
To get out of the building.
They screamed and screamed and screamed
For themselves, their families and friends.
They cried and cried and cried
It happened so quickly.
It happened so fast
They were the Twin Towers.

Sarah Carpenter (11)
Sawston Village College

MY FIRST SIX DAYS AT SAWSTON

Big buildings shadowing Sawston,
Paths full of students rushing like the cars on the A14
Year 11s strutting around not minding that they're bumping into us
Teachers walking, watching for collars
One person telling you to put it in, one person out
Everyone, even teachers, waiting for break
To fill up like cars filling up with petrol
A playground the size of the moon at night
Dodging balls flying at you from all directions
Lessons before lunch so short, but seem so long
Going to a different lesson, I wish I had a car.

Luke Tancock (11)
Sawston Village College

FEAR

Fear is a snaring trap
A hunter with no shape
Fear is a terrible beast
Which lurks in the deep
Fear tricks, traps and destroys
Fear is a monster, ancient yet young
Fear is a bow, old but deadly strung
Fear can roar and rage
And be as gentle as a mouse
Fear is the monster under the bed
Fear is the iceberg on a dark and moonless night
Fear is the ghost in the ancient house
Fear is the scritch scratch in a dark attic
But fear always comes to one thing
And that is death
And the only cure is hope.

Euan Bright (11)
Sawston Village College

FALLING LEAVES

F un is coming
A utumn running
L oving autumn
L oving the breeze
I n and out the trees
N eeding to wear a hat and coat
G rinning as they go

L eaves flowing
E veryone is coming
A lways floating this way and that
V ery cold and wet
E very day now
S ummer is over.

Charlotte Levien (11)
Sawston Village College

CAR DREAMS

Four wheels that's all I could see,
Fast or what, I wish that was me.
The roar of the engine, rubber burning,
Leaves me with a dreadful yearning.
A body kit sleek and shining,
Leather and walnut for the lining,
Spoilers, alloys, dump valves and more,
This mean motor could never bore,
One day she will be mine,
But for now I must pine,
Gone, only a cloud of dust to see,
For the moment, that's good enough for me.

Mark Leaney (14)
Sawston Village College

POWER?

Waiting
Crawling
Sneaking
Growing
Fear me
For I am you
Love me
For I am great
Cower from me
For I can destroy you
Come before me
For I shall praise you
If you are
Then you can see
The ice and the fire
Become one
And shining
In the sky
Knowing I can win
And be
Power itself
But the greater
Will always be
Above me
And seeing
Everything.

Fraser Clark (13)
Sawston Village College

LONE WOLF

Will I be forgotten?
Will they come back?
Will they be too busy
To rescue me from this pitch-black?

I am all alone,
A lone wolf,
Trapped in this world,
Unknown to the human race,
Ancient and old.

I hear the planes overhead,
The bombs going off.
Am I too close to them?
Will they finish me off?

As I cough and splutter
In this ancient land,
I hear a drone close by,
A bomb about to land.

I hear a siren howling,
Or is it in my soul?
My problem's deep inside me,
Buried in a hole.

A bomb about to land on me,
There's nothing more to say,
I've struggled on and on,
But that's the end of today.

Chloë Hamilton (11)
Sawston Village College

MY FIRST SIX WEEKS AT SAWSTON

Sitting on the bus
So many people that look like me
But not nearly as nervous
I'm the stranger on the bus
They know each other
I don't

First day - assembly
Talks about getting to know people
Everyone else knows people across the aisle
I don't

Form room
My two best friends
At last
Someone I know

Break time
Relief - my friends at last
People I feel that I can talk to

Lessons
Science - I try to concentrate
I can't
My mind's somewhere else

Lunchtime
Chaos in the queue
Get my lunch
Hot food
Sit and talk with friends
I feel like we're back at primary school again

More lessons
The rest of the school's here
Noise and people everywhere
Music
Maths
We've completed the work, wait for the bell.

The bell's gone
In the bus queues
Very crowded and noisy

Follow people to the bus
Sit down
The bus takes us home
I get off at my stop
Walk home

At home
Done my homework
Think about the day
It wasn't all that bad
I could get used to it.

Charlotte Bransfield-Garth (12)
Sawston Village College

IN MY ROOM

In my room there are secrets,
In my room there are treasures,
In my room there are ghosts,
In my room there are monsters,
In my room there are ghouls
And in my room there is my sister,
The scariest one of them all!

Mark Gorringe (11)
Sawston Village College

THE SHOP WINDOWS

I walked up the road,
glaring in the windows.
I looked through the bakers to see all the food,
I looked in the toy shop and saw all the kids.
I turned my head to the left of the shops,
There was the bank and the post office,
People walking in and out.
I turned my head to the front this time,
Then I saw the brand new shop 'Pet Shop'.
I ran and ran as fast as I could
And there inside I could see all sorts of pets to choose from.
Cats, kittens, dogs, puppies, fish, hamsters, rabbits and more,
Every day I went to the pet shop to play with the animals,
What better thing to do?

Tanya Browne (11)
Sawston Village College

WHAT AM I?

I come in all these shapes and sizes
And all those funky colours.
Most people have me in white.
I can be big, I can be small,
You can also extend me.
Some people take care of me,
Some people treat me like a dump.
I can be for sale,
I can be for rent,
Either one, I am very expensive.
What am I?

Deniz Mehmet (11)
Sawston Village College

IF ONLY I HAD A HEART

The sun's darkness is shining upon me,
The darkness of my soul is taking control over me.
It is suspicious, sinister and cold.
My mind is crying for help.
My mind is asking for pain.
I can hardly breathe.
I need help, I need help now!
Everything around me is so chaotic,
Everything around me is just emptiness.
Existence itself is begging for pain.
Existence itself is asking for help.
Help!
Help!
If only I had a heart . . .
But if I had a heart, it would break my chest.

Sarah Pouele (14)
Sawston Village College

WEEPING WILLOW

Weeping willow with your tears running down,
Why do you always weep and frown?
Is it because they loved you one day,
Is it because they could not stay?
Are your branches where they would swing?
Do you long for the happiness that day would bring?
They found shelter in your shade,
Did you think their laughter would never fade?
Weeping willow stop your tears,
There is something to calm your fears.
Do you think that death will ever part?
Every way they know they'll always be in your heart!

Stephanie Casey (11)
Sawston Village College

THE FOOTBALL HOOLIGAN

He has a great, shiny, bald head
And wants the opposing team dead.
He stands with a brick in one hand,
Whilst he rips off the seats from the stand.
His IQ is about 25,
It's a wonder he is still alive.
He is an England nutter,
Who drains all his sorrows in the gutter.
He is racist and swears all the time,
He's always committing a crime.
Even in the cold, he wears shorts,
That's when he isn't in court.
Battle scars cover his face,
The local is his stupid gang's base.
The chant that he shouts is absurd
And is made up of four-letter words.
On one arm he has a tattoo,
He beats his wife black and blue.

Jonathan Davies (13)
Sawston Village College

LEAP LIKE A LEOPARD

Leap like a leopard,
Crawl like a snail,
Prowl like a tiger,
Swim like a whale.

Miaow like a kitten,
Bark like a dog,
Moo like a cow,
Jump like a frog.

Howl like a wolf,
Purr like a cat,
Slither like a snake,
Scamper like a rat.

Sam Coupland (11)
Sawston Village College

SECONDARY SCHOOL

Everyone walking,
    All the same,
        Going the same way
    Looking the same.
Like sheep we wander
    Follow the crowd,
        Where are we gong?
    Was that the bell?
Better look in our timetables.
    OK, It's music, maths, then science.
        Everyone's late,
    It's just history, then break!
I won't make it that far!
    I'll die before I get out,
        Help me!
    Help me!
Aah!
    I'm out,
        I'm free!
Throughout the day,
    Everyone knew
        That the best part of school is . . .
    Home time!

Rebecca Nunn (11)
Sawston Village College

My Six Weeks At Sawston

The heavens grew with rage
As I neared the school gates.
My heart was racing like a tornado
Everyone stuck together like bread and butter.
A timetable. What for?
Most lessons were quite new.
All teachers with a smiling face
Homework was worst of all.
Maths, science, French and English
Not fair.

Ahh! Lunch at long last.
Two lessons to go, then all over.
It took forever for time to go.
When I heard the bell go
I jumped for joy.
Home at last.

Pamela Akita (11)
Sawston Village College

See

See the child,
She lived on the street.
See the warmth,
She lived in a dump.
See the man,
He wandered, drunk.
See the boy,
He lived on his own.
See the birds,
Perched on their headstones.

Rachel Danes (14)
Sawston Village College

THE WORLD

A ll the animals of the Earth are in pain,
From human greed for land to gain.

N asty hunters come and shoot the beasts,
Threatening all animals with being eaten as a feast.

I n this beautiful world God created,
Humans have destroyed, killed and mutilated.

M any humans throw rubbish and waste,
Ruining the countryside in our haste.

A nimals' habitats from burrows to trees,
Are being demolished for man's own needs.

L ucky for animals, some people doing good,
Protecting the environment as best they could.

S ome humans will never learn that animals need caring,
Because God only created the world for peace and sharing.

Sarah Pride (12)
Sawston Village College

A RAINY DAY

As the last speck of sunshine fades in the sky,
The rain starts to fall from way up high.

The leaves start to shiver as the wind rushes in,
The rain falls hard with the thunder and lightning.

But as it's getting worse, the clouds start to part
And the sunshine hits you like a deadly dart.

Rosie McLaughlin (13)
Sawston Village College

MEMORIES

Good memories, bad memories,
What memories do you have?
Memories can make you smile
At the great times you have had.
Memories of you and your friends,
Playing in the playground when you were small
Are just a few you may never forget.

Sometimes memories are bad,
From having an accident
To losing a relative or a close friend,
These are memories you would rather forget.
Bad memories are kept locked away
Until one day, you suddenly remember them.
Remembering bad memories makes you sad and cry,
But then the good memories make you smile and be happy.

So remember all the great times
As they are memories that last.

Shona Rookes (14)
Sawston Village College

DARK NIGHT

Night is dark and day is light,
Dark is dingy and day is bright.
Dark is like a black dye
Which clears in the morning
When it's dawning.
Day and night are like a light
Being turned on and off.

Chris Gatward (12)
Sawston Village College

IS HE THE ONE FOR ME?

He steps from the depths of our minds,
making our hearts flutter.
The mind's eye goes cloudy and all is a whirl.

Puzzling thoughts swim in our minds,
making us say those important words.
Fiery are our hearts when we think of him.

Questions leading to questions,
leaping over answers and making them a muddle.

Our mind may say no, but our heart says yes.
Right or wrong may this be, but we leap in,
just to see.

The whirling mists are at last all gone
and now we can again see clear.

Right or wrong may the answer be,
but now I know that he's for me.

Victoria Brown (13)
Sawston Village College

NIGHT POEM

The sky was
a black bat,
soaring through the sky,
with a spotted front.
It swooped throughout the night,
backwards and forwards,
until morning came.

Grant Anderson (13)
Sawston Village College

IF

If you look up at the sky at night,
All you see is a blackie-blue background
With silver and gold sparkles.
It's not just that. (Read on)

Mice creeping around dark alleys,
Open expanse of sparkling stuff,
Overflow of water dripping from the gutter,
Noises of creatures crawling around,
Singing of crickets,
Silent stars,
Twittering of small insects' feet,
A cute tabby cat walking along a wall,
Rolls of spiders' webs strung everywhere.
Soon it will be day.

Wherever you are,
Just look up at the night sky.
Look, listen for all these things.

Charlotte Coulson (13)
Sawston Village College

THE DANCING BEAR

You prance and twirl to please a crowd
Full of jeering faces,
All of them laughing out loud.

Heavy chains and metal rods
Beat your feet for two pence
And silver pennies.

The people care nothing for your pain and suffering.
You live in a cold cruel world where nobody cares.
You are hungry and weak,
You are the dancing bear.

Maria Reali (12)
Sawston Village College

POEM?

Teacher said, 'Write a poem,'
But I really don't know how.
I really need a subject,
I really need it now!

Should I write a couplet or
Should I write a limerick?
I really don't know what to write,
I really need it quick!

Should I ask a poet?
Should I ask a pro?
A famous Booker prizewinner?
I don't know where to go!

Should I ask the audience?
Should I phone a friend?
I can't go 50/50,
This really is the end.

This poem is a disaster,
It really hurts my head,
I'll probably have to scrap it.
I think I'll go to bed.

Matthew Swain (13)
Sawston Village College

NIGHT POEM

In my gentle rest I lie half asleep, half awake, listening to
the sounds of the wind gently rustling the trees. I feel peaceful.

The owls hoot reassuringly and the crickets chirp as though snoring.
The street lamps illuminate the empty streets.

Miaow! An alley cat falls from a dustbin, shell-shocked and
covered in potato peelings. It stalks off, cursing in its head.

Families are curled up on the sofas, watching the evening entertainment
with a cup of cocoa and biscuits.

A fire roars as an old dear falls peacefully to sleep in front of it,
not knowing that she will never wake.

A workaholic sits until dawn signing papers and yelling at others
like him, hoping it will ease the pain when he gets home
with no one to greet him or make him feel loved.

A tramp on London's underground struggles to stay awake and
play the last few notes on his guitar, just to earn a few more pennies.

As I drift off into a soft, silent slumber, I think about
everyone around the world, what they are doing and then . . .

Nicola Simmons (12)
Sawston Village College

NIGHT POEM

Evening comes and shadows fall,
The hoot of an owl as it gives a call,
Darkness is creeping all around
Till the moonbeams fall onto the ground.
Little diamonds twinkle so bright
In the heavens of the night.

Tom Foote (12)
Sawston Village College

GHOSTS

No one believes in them but you,
You can sense their evil presence when you are alone,
Their icy breath whispers down your back,
Making the hairs on your neck stand on end.

The smell of fear indicates that they are closing in on you,
Poisoning your mind and devouring your soul.
You ask yourself,
Have they come to seek revenge?

Is there some unknown secret that I was not aware of?
Have I done anything wrong?
Is someone trying to tell me a message,
Or is it all in my head?

John Connellan (14)
Sawston Village College

BLITZ

I saw the planes,
I saw them fall,
I heard the explosions,
Then I heard silence.

Another town flattened,
A community destroyed,
Hundreds of deaths
And yet, no satisfaction.

Elaine Paterson (13)
Sawston Village College

THOUGHT

I stare out of the window into the never-ending darkness,
The moon glows big and bright
And just a small crack of light floods the floor.
This is my time.
Nobody knows what I'm thinking right now, they never will.
Nobody understands me, I don't understand them.
Everybody's changed,
They all seem so distant.
I wish things could be the way they used to be,
I wish the world wasn't so messed up,
I wish I didn't feel so empty inside
And sometimes, I wish I could fly away . . .

Harriet Richmond (13)
Sawston Village College

A POEM

In my room there is a
bed.
In my room there is a
set of shelves.
In my room there is a
shelf for all my special things.
In my room there is a
train track.
In my room there is a
wardrobe.
In my room there is
nothing now!

Thomas Bex (11)
Sawston Village College

IN MY BEDROOM

In my bedroom there is
a biting bed.
In my bedroom there is
a dancing chair.
In my bedroom there is
a singing toy box.
In my bedroom there is
a violent computer.
In my bedroom there is
a roaring printer.
In my bedroom there is
a sparkling light bulb.
In my bedroom there's everything,
But me.

Joseph Ash (11)
Sawston Village College

SNATCHED

One step,
Sixty seconds,
Abducted.

Six months,
Anguish,
Found,
Murdered.

Adele Whitby (14)
Sawston Village College

SECRETS

Secrets
Are the things that lie in my room.
Secrets,
The things that only I know.
Secrets,
Of feelings, memories and the past.
Secrets
Are buried deep in my soul.
Secrets,
Things you can never run from.
Secrets,
Things that will never be gone.

Louisa Hodge (11)
Sawston Village College

THE STORY OF MY LIFE

As he walked into the room,
It was like a big light turned on inside my heart,
A smile on a miserable face,
A sign of hope in an empty world.
But then I see him
Smile at another girl,
Walk over and hug her.
No light, no smile, no hope
For me,
Forever.

Emily Brisley (14)
Sawston Village College

NIGHT

I can feel his cold, clammy hands
tugging at my clothes and around my neck.
He is pulling me down, suffocating me
in a never-ending pool of darkened dreams,
catching the breath in my lungs.
He is moving faster and faster,
enveloping all that represents love and happiness
in a deathly blanket.
All I can hear is the slow, steady beating
of my clockwork heart.
Minutes stumble by like hours and
still he stays, winking his milky eye,
the only light in the dead, frozen room.
Just when I give up all hope of morning,
bright beams of sunshine dance across my window sill
then flood the room, killing him,
killing him at least until tonight.

Frances Sawcer (13)
Sawston Village College

MY ROOM

My room is full of memories,
My room is my pirate ship,
My room is a wonderful room of fun and laughter,
My room is my closest friend when I am troubled,
My room is my castle,
My room is my favourite.

Nathan Whitaker (11)
Sawston Village College

A Sunset's Eve

As the temperature slowly cooled,
A light, fresh breeze swept upon my sun-kissed face.
The chirping and delightful noises of children and animals
Filled me with a warm glow inside.
The pastel shades of a breath-taking sky
Were a unique sight
As they reflected onto the green and blue ocean.
It glistened like a firework on a winter's night.
The huge fireball slowly faded away into the distance,
Each time I blinked, the sun became further away.
It flickered as it hid away in the distance.
Suddenly, the warmth and brightness had turned
Into a cool, clear night.
All I could do now was to wait through the night
Until tomorrow,
Another peaceful day,
Make this last.

Emily Lloyd-Ruck (13)
Sawston Village College

Night Poem

The night spreads across the sky,
a tide of darkness,
Like the sea,
Covering everything in its path,
Blocking the sunlight
From the earth below.
Stays till morning,
Leaving like a receding wave,
Gone, but to return.

James Tofts (13)
Sawston Village College

EVACUEE

I'm on the train from King's Cross Station,
I really want to get there, but I still am patient.
I've packed my shrapnel and air rifle,
Looking at my packed lunch, yes! Strawberry trifle.
I've been on the train now for five hours,
Out of the window I see these strange new flowers,
Never seen so much green before
And trees the size of a giant's front door.
On my left this huge dog goes, *moan!*
Over to the right, the sea so blue.
I get off the train to a whole new world,
The family that collect me have a son called Harold.
I like the family and they have a wicked, huge house,
But I do miss my mum and Steve, my pet mouse.

Martin Ball (13)
Sawston Village College

THE ANTS

The night creeps in like a row of ants
Scattering all over the place,
Climbing up and down,
Going in different directions,
Making no sound at all.
Colder and colder,
Darker and darker,
Ending the day so fast
And getting ready
To start anew.

Lewis Cornwell (12)
Sawston Village College

NIGHT-TIME

A s night-time falls the world changes
T o a spooky and mysterious place;

N othing is safe from the night and the surprises it'll bring.
I ce and frost bite at the world attacking all it can.
G listening stars light the world like little angels from above.
H uge curtains draw around the Earth, holding in the darkness.
T omorrow seems so far away.

T rees' skeletons dance around in the shadows,
I nviting spirits to come and play.
M agnificent cobwebs sparkle in the moonlight;
E verything is alive.

Helen Cottle (13)
Sawston Village College

JOB INTERVIEWS

Tick-tock, tick-tock,
The time drags on.
The grilling had finished,
He said to wait outside,
The interview was over.
What would be the outcome?
He walked out of his office
And looked in my direction.
He raised his arm and beckoned me over.
'The job is yours.'
Nervousness over!

Hannah Griggs (14)
Sawston Village College

WHAT'S IN MY CUPBOARD?

There's something in my cupboard,
But I don't know what.
There's something in my cupboard
And it smells like rot.

Should I open it, or should I not?
There might be a monster, which will gobble me up.
Should I say hello, or should I leave it alone?

There's something in my cupboard but I don't know what.
If I disturb it, it might get mad or
It might be as friendly as a cat.

I open it and it comes out and . . .
'Hello,' said the monster and
He's now my best friend.

Danielle Graham (11)
Sawston Village College

TICK-TOCK CLOCK

As my tummy rumbles,
The maths teacher groans and mumbles.
Everyone watches the clock,
They gasp at every tick-tock.
The work is not done,
But my bag weighs a tonne.
I can never find a smile,
I want to run a mile.
The bell finally rings,
Everyone prays and sings,
Only another five lessons to go.

Aaron Wakefield (13)
Sawston Village College

THE PAIN OF VICTORY

On the starting line
The pounding heartbeat drowns out the distant crowd,
The tense body is apprehensive for the gun.
As the smoking gun fires
The body jolts into action,
The heaving crowd begins to roar.
You and the opposition -
What opposition?
Pain.
With the bitter wind whistling through the air,
The burning lungs start to labour.
All around is silent,
Save the hungry breathing.
As the top bend approaches
The legs move faster,
Springing and ploughing up the worn turf.
Now the battle with pain as the home straight appears,
Hoards of supporters line the track,
You're trying to beat the tortured legs,
The shouting hits you like waves on the shore.
Can you bear the pain?
The finish line approaches,
Just a few more strides,
You're reaching for the line -
Yes!
Relief.
You're gasping for breath,
Your legs turn to jelly,
The pain of victory.

William Atkinson (13)
Sawston Village College

WHO'S THERE?

Who's there when . . .
You are awaiting a world of dreams
And you feel a slight brush on your fingertips?

Who's there when . . .
The night is creeping all around you
With pure darkness lurking in the shadows?

Who's there when . . .
The wind is howling through the trees
And the distant whisper overwhelms your senses?

Who's there?
Could be many things.
All can be explained,
But this cannot.

Who's there?
I am
And so is something,
Everything
Ancient,
Young,
Powerful,
Weak,
Light,
Dark,
Good,
Evil.

Megan Saunders (13)
Sawston Village College

DREAMS AND CHANCES

A wisp of white,
A puff of smoke,
A large and pearly cloud.
Castles in the moonlight
And spaceships in the sky.
Palaces made of chocolate
And rivers made of cream.
If only, if only these were all true,
But no, it's just a dream.

Roll of thunder
In the sky,
Clouds of rain
Fall brown and dry.
Monsters, spiders, dark, black death,
Just one last chance,
Just one last breath.

Susannah Bangham (13)
Sawston Village College

BULLY

Kid-kicker,
Child-scarer,
Children-beater,
Sibling-hunter,
That's one heck of a bully.

Kirstie Facer (11)
Sawston Village College

DREAMING LUCIDLY OF LOVE?

I find myself staring across the room
And listening as she sings in blissful tune.
Like heavenly angels singing on high,
A white heart of innocence, pure like mine.
Free as a dove, unknown to woes of love.

I'm dreaming lucidly of her and me,
Ever together for eternity.
Her warm, light brown eyes, beautiful, perfect.
Her soft, brown hair: a man's hand intersect.
His arms embracing her, she kisses back.

A sharp shock of lightning goes straight through me,

I was wrong! And in that precise moment
When I lost that important component,
My secret love, did my life destroy.

David Sampson (16)
Stanground College

THE WIND IN MANY COLOURS

I see the wind in many colours,
Snowflake blue and ice cream white,
It fills and splashes into every gap,
Marking the land in its own silent way.
Touching our cheeks with rosy red,
And making us glow inside
All of this from something so simple
The wind.

Charlotte Morris (12)
The Perse School For Girls

FRIENDS

Good friends are like bottles.
You can tell them your secrets and they store them like glass bottles.

Sometimes the bottles smash and spill whispers and giggles
On to the floor for just anybody to sweep up.

But the best friends are the ones that lock your secrets away like wine
Bottles in a dark, dusty cellar, because then when the bottle is
Carefully opened, what's inside is all the more precious.

Ellen Pilsworth (13)
The Perse School For Girls

MIDNIGHT

Midnight and all is quiet.
The streets, so full by day, are empty now.
The shops locked up, their keepers home in bed,
The world asleep, oblivious.
Yet somewhere, in a back street, lies a child.
Too cold to sleep, too tired to wake,
Huddled on a piece of sacking.
No home in which to spend the winter days,
No possessions, to while away the time,
No family or friends to comfort them,
No life to live, no future.
Midnight and all is quiet.
We lie asleep, yet somewhere cries a child.

Susanna Bridge (12)
The Perse School For Girls

THE KITE

A
kite
drifting lazily through
the tremendous azure sky. The
fluffy white clouds sailed peacefully,
lingering against the sun. The boy and the kite
went into the house as the sun sank
behind hills laden with
flourishing flowers
and plants.
The
stars
and
the
moon
put   came
to   are   sheepishly
bed.   kite   out
the   as
and   the
boy

Collette Dampier (12)
The Perse School For Girls

A TREE HAIKU

I stand up here tall,
My proud face hidden by leaves,
My mind, all alone.

Abi Stacey (11)
The Perse School For Girls

THE TREE SPEAKS

For me,
Life is like a film,
Rolling on forever.
I've seen all the best-sellers,
Drama, comedy, romance, mystery,
Your cartoon figures,
Race the scenes away.
The rolls of film growing,
Like my withered trunk,
No more Bagpuss,
James Bond and his new sports car.

For me,
Life is like a book,
A never-ending diary:
Worries, secrets, jokes,
Your pencilled outlines
Dream the words away,
The pages falling,
Like my autumn leaves.
My stories
Beyond your imagination.

For me,
Life's been uprooted.
I've walked the world
Of all your minds,
I feel lifted from the ground,
Not cluttered in a forest,
Or clumped in a hedgerow,
Chopped for paper,
Or carved for your homes.
My life is the school,
The school's life is mine.

Claire Judd (11)
The Perse School For Girls

ON MY OWN

My days are numbered,
I know it in my heart,
I just want to step back,
Let my life depart,
I want to die, but I can't.

I'm on my own, not a soul enters my room,
I am lying awake,
Overpowered with doom,
Every breath I take could be my last.

The world around me starts to merge into one,
My eyes start to close,
My breathing is slow,
I am drifting away into a land of sorrow.

There's a *bang*, a *crash*,
My eyes snap open,
I can see a figure,
No words are spoken.

I am not alone,
I am found,
I am free.

I will leave my world of nothing,
I will rise up to meet the sun,
My loneliness now leaves me,
My life has re-begun.

Anna Taylor (12)
The Perse School For Girls

THE VOICE OF THE TREE

I whisper my secrets to the world,
My voice carried away on the breeze.
The girls walk past unknowing,
Unhearing, not listening to the trees.

I lower my leaves to the children,
I raise my leaves to the birds,
I stretch my boughs to the classrooms
Yet still I remain unheard.

And as the sun is setting
And the day draws to an end,
My questions remain unanswered,
I am still without a friend.

Then the moon shines above me,
She is silent, but she is kind.
She too cannot say
What is troubling her mind.

And then the sun starts rising
And waking up the men.
I hear the city noises
And my troubles start again.

Gemma Bowes (11)
The Perse School For Girls

SPEECH

Slowly, silently with the wind I sway,
When even the slightest breeze comes my way,
One by one my leaves float away,
Leaving me here, with nothing more to say.

Anisha Lakhani (12)
The Perse School For Girls

NATURE

The cool wind ruffles my hair,
It's like a voice whispering in my ear
I see the tree's branches swaying like waves
I see the tree's crisp leaves falling to the ground.
The leaves float, as if on clouds,
Slowly falling down and down.
They land on the jewelled grass, without a sound.
The grass is now iced with leaves and conkers.
I kick a conker and its shell splits open,
The precious stone has been found
And it rolls along the ground.
It lands on the damp, warm soil of a flowerbed
Purple, white, orange and red;
All these colours bring me to life,
As if I was caught in a dream
I walk along the bank, the leaves crunching under me
I walk to the river, an ocean, yet a trickling stream
The water flows in one direction
Its rippling waters pass me by
And never come to an end . . .

I look around me, watching the life that does not live:
The wind, the grass, the river, the trees
Everything around me stirs in the breeze
I find my voice
And whisper,
'Thank you.'
The wind carries my prayer, far, far away.
I think Nature heard me
I think Nature knows me.

Emily Pickup (12)
The Perse School For Girls

CHANGED

The wild water has been stilled,
the wind in the trees has fallen,
the sun has sunk deep into the dusk,
everything has changed.

The birds have shed all their feathers,
the animals individual scents have blurred into one,
the fish are floating lifelessly,
everything has changed.

The smell of the spring grass has faded,
the feel of soft hair has lost its touch,
the noise made by the seagulls shrieking has been quietened,
everything has changed.

The love of my life has been taken away from me,
everything has changed.

Elizabeth McLaren (13)
The Perse School For Girls

A TREE SPEAKS

As I walked outside one day,
I heard a voice call out and say,
'Can you guess what I have seen?
My knowledge beats an Einstein keen.'

As I walked outside one day,
I heard a voice call out and say,
'Can you guess what I have smelt?
Some of the things they make me melt.'

As I walked outside one day,
I heard a voice call out and say,
'Can you guess what I have felt?
The worries of a child, a problem undealt.'

And I replied, 'I cannot say I can
What have you felt and what have you smelt?
And what have you seen, I wish I could have been
There to share it with you.'

Zosia Krasodomska-Jones (11)
The Perse School For Girls

I SEE...

I see everything that is happy
Small children playing in the garden
People splashing in the sea
The hustle of the marketplace
Everybody smiling and laughing.

I see everything that is sad
People dying of hunger
Everybody fighting each other
Losing that special family member
Everybody dismal and lonely.

I see everything that is tranquil
Clear water in the stream
The still rainforest
An elephant alone on the African plain
Everything peaceful and calm
But I, the sun, still shine on everyone.

Hannah Gray (12)
The Perse School For Girls

THE TREE THAT DREAMS

I feel the rushing wind
On my branches
The cool breeze
My companion when others
Have deserted me.

To them I am an object,
A thing,
To be pretty and
Entertaining when they
Want it.

I am lonely,
I call out in despair
No one hears,
No one cares,
I have no hope they will.

I have tried to please them,
They do not notice
How hard I try
To help them and
Be free of *The Thought.*

The Thought of being lost,
Lost on a wide, open ocean,
Drifting on my own
Seeing others together,
Laughing, crying - together.

Oh how I wish I
Could join them!
I will never speak
A word - I promise
Only let me be with you.

You need not
Talk to me,
Just treat me with
Respect and love
And do not forget me.

Together we will conquer
The world!
We will win and lose,
But together
We will laugh at all.

No, that will never be,
I hope one day
Someone will come
And help me,
But all I have is hope.

One cannot put all
Their trust in *Hope* alone
One must act
And trust no one,
Not even thyself.

So I stand here still
Shading my past with my leaves
I love to rustle with
The moonlight and the
Wind - I wait for you still.

Veronica Andersson (13)
The Perse School For Girls

I DREAMED A DREAM

I thought I dreamed a dream of a lady gone and been
A lady lovely, a lady jolly
So I strolled into that dream.

I was walking in the woods one day and gladly lost my way
Then I came across my heart, the heart I lose too soon!
That lady bright, that lady right
Too beautiful to be true.

The drums sounded, the dream faded
And real life is back at my door, I dreamt of more
But nothing came to mind.

I know I loved that lady, but before I've left the world
I know I'll see that lady and be with her for evermore.

Nicole Shui (12)
The Perse School For Girls

I DREAM TOO MUCH

I dream of my horse listening to me.
I dream of not pulling her back, I wish she was weaker.
I dream of putting in a stronger bit to control her.
I dream of racing her on a track.
I dream of winning when she has tried.

I dream of galloping away as fast as I can.
I dream of jumping and racing with the wind.
I dream of being left alone with my friends.
I dream of a tasty feather bit to pull on my mouth.
I dream of not being locked up in a cold stable.
I dream of my family.
    To be free.

Francesca Freeman (12)
The Perse School For Girls

THE TREE

The tree has been sitting alone
For centuries on end
No one thought to love him
Or call him their good friend
All he needs is a little bit
Of friendliness, respect and care,
But on no occasion someone
Even acts as though he's there
Sometimes he hopes that someone
Will notice him and see
That his branches and flowers
Are wonderful and free
But then he thinks again
As he stands there on his own
Nobody will ever treasure him
He will forever be alone.

Lauren Churchman (11)
The Perse School For Girls

THE TRICKLE

Dancing in the moonlight
The shimmering water
Drifting down the valley
Suddenly it *stops*.

Pebbles, stones, even gold!
Trickling slowly from the streams
Was that a sparkle of light?
The glimmer of a mystery lost in the tide.

Henrietta Lawrence (12)
The Perse School For Girls

MIDNIGHT IN THE GARDEN

When the dark of night
Starts to creep
And shadows lurk in the midnight air
The tree comes to life.

I remember the little girl
Planting the seedling
When the world was grey and dull
And there was no life.

She came to visit me every day
And due to her love I grew
She watered and fed me by herself
There was nothing she wouldn't do for me.

Then she stopped coming
Where she was I never knew
I carried on though she never came
And here I am today.

She will never come back
For I have lost all hope.
The tree sighs and goes to sleep
Ready for another day.

In the morning the tree stirs
And watches the little children
Running and playing under its branches
It stands there and waits.

In the mid afternoon
When families start to go home
The tree relaxes and starts to talk
To itself.

And then I see her, I see her
Running over the plain.
She's come back for me
I will never be alone again.

And so the tree and the girl
Are happily reunited
She comes to visit it every day
And the tree's memories relive.

Ankaret Fillipich (11)
The Perse School For Girls

THE SEA

I whisper night and day
Through all my waves
But no one ever listens.

Sometimes I get very angry
Because I am hungry
For someone to listen to me.

Sometimes I am calm
When I feel that someone's as soothing as balm
But then I wonder, how can this be?

I have no friends
But somehow someone mends
All my wounds.

I don't know who it is
I have no one to quiz,
But maybe somewhere there is a friend for me.

Catherina Yurchyshyn (12)
The Perse School For Girls